How to Get Rich

Business Lessons From The Bible

URIAH BEADLE

HOW TO GET RICH

BUSINESS LESSONS FROM THE BIBLE

Belknap & Poole
Publishers
New York

DEDICATION

This book is dedicated to you. The business person working for something as rare as steady growth, the entrepreneur hoping to find a new way to create wealth, or the freelancer fighting for a more stable prosperity. You are heroic.

I will never be able to highly enough praise the amount of courage it takes to do what you do: To wake up every day and work for your own wellbeing in the face of all the adversity in the world, despite the economic giants that lurk on the landscape, with so many temptations set in our path…To try for success while remaining a morally upright individual is increasingly difficult.

Christianity demands a huge amount of sacrifice of its practitioners. That's why so few in the world are truly good Christians. And yet, still, so many of you strive to be so. This book is dedicated to you.

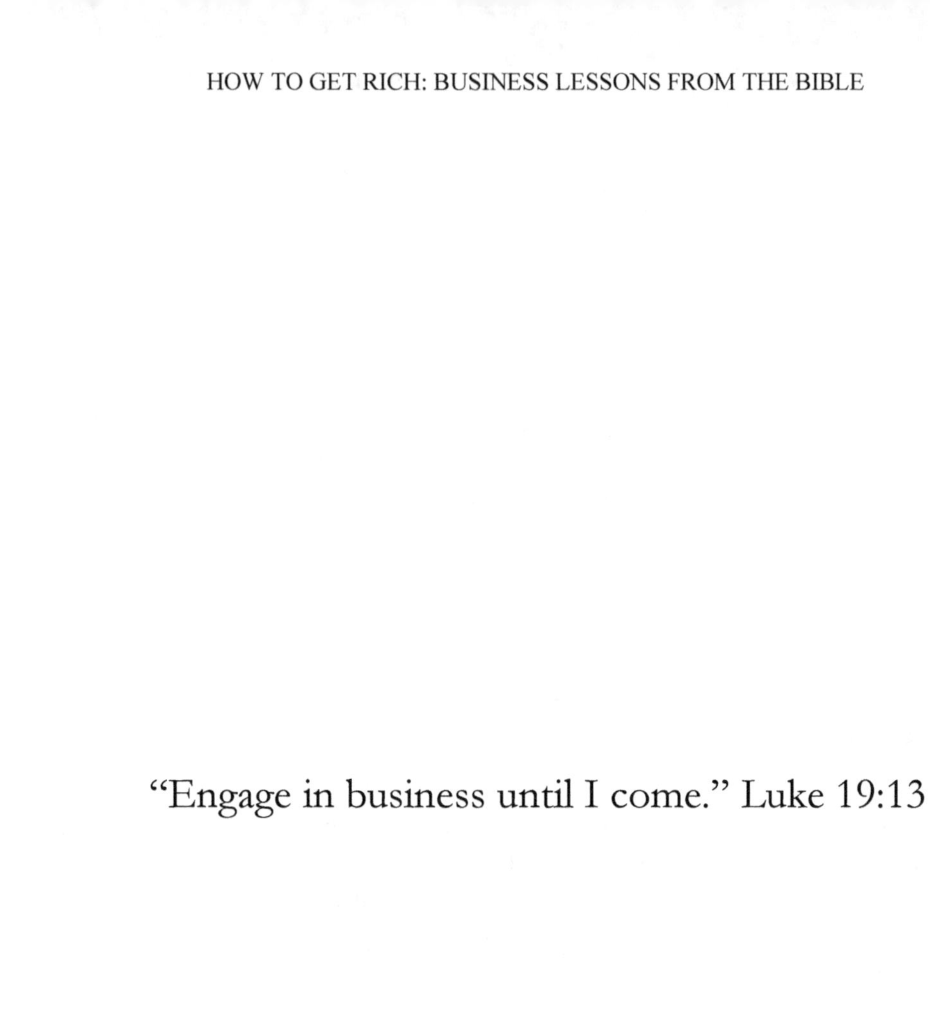

"Engage in business until I come." Luke 19:13

CONTENTS

"Great is our Lord, his understanding is beyond measure." Psalm 147:5

INTRODUCTION

The Holy Bible is more than a divinely inspired book; it is God's guide to life. It is an instruction manual. God willed for it to contain an all-encompassing treasury of His comprehensive wisdom. Consequently, within the realm of God's wisdom rests divinely authenticated best-business practices.

When I was approached to write this book - which is based on my lecture series - it was of paramount importance that the final product be not only for Christians, but for anyone who seeks to increase their wealth.

As a result, this exegetical book is not about religion or the power of faith, this is about business practices. Business practices based on narratives from the Bible, and, therefore rooted in the comprehensive wisdom of God.

If you believe the Holy Bible is the source of absolute truth, then you must also believe that the business lessons contained within the Bible were put there by God for us to learn from. Plainly, I believe everything in the Bible was put there by God for us to learn from.

Some stories in the Bible are cautionary tales where we are supposed to learn how "not" to behave, but still others - and this is *many* stories - depict people and situations that are absolutely 100% relevant to an understanding of our modern lives, and our modern business lives in particular.

Consider this fact; while there are around 500 verses in the Bible about Faith and Prayer, there are 2,350 Bible verses about money. Why was money such a concern in Biblical times? For the same reason money is a concern today: This is life on Earth! Money is necessary and business people make money. Plainly put, in our modern world, money allows life to continue. This is what God wants.

So please read this book, study its lessons and make your money. It is my prayer that the following lessons will increase your wealth and enrich your faith.

"An intelligent heart acquires knowledge, and the ear of the wise seeks knowledge." Psalm 119:105

PART 1

Divine Business Skills

Some of the wealthiest people in human history are featured well and praised for their good deeds in the Holy Bible. Seeing the Bible through a modern lens such as our business life enriches your connection to the Holy Word. Reading the Bible through a business lens is an illuminating way to learn valuable money-making lessons. Here, we begin...

ABRAHAM

Abraham is now known as the Patriarch of three major religions, Judaism, Islam, and Christianity. But his life story begins as Abram in a polytheistic Mesopotamia. One of the main business lessons of Abram's life is that he was never satisfied with the world that he was born into.

Abram was a change-maker for whom "good enough" was never "enough." He questioned everything about the world where he was born and even the family business into which he was apprenticed. Like many iconoclasts, Abram's father Terah was different, he was the kind of man who settled.

The word Terah means "delay" or "wanderer." By counter-example, Terah set Abraham on a course to break from his father and break from all that his family had known. It is only by risking great failure that we can achieve great success.

The Bible tells us that Terah's profession was making religious devotional statues for the moon goddess Ningal's temple complex. Archeology proves that these statues were often copper or bronze. That he would move his family to Harran, in the hills north of Canaan makes sense in light of this because Harran was the center of Ningal's cult within the Hittite Empire.

But as a worker of the metallurgical trade, Terah would not have prayed to Ningal, but instead, he would have prayed to a metallurgical deity. As one living within the Hittite Empire, it may have been Hasameli. However, the neighboring Greek pantheon had a similar god called

Hephaestus, his Roman equivalent was Vulcan. These metallurgical gods were all associated with volcanic descriptions which closely mirror the smoke, fire, black slag and molten red metal produced in the smelting process. Every pantheon had a god of metallurgy, even the Canaanite pantheon.

The Bible tells us that Terah wanted to lead his family to the land of Canaan, a place famous for the copper mines of Timna in the Negev Valley.

"But when they came to Harran, they settled there"
Genesis 11:31.

Not a change-maker like his son, Terah settled in Harran. Harran was the land of comfort, but Canaan was the land of promise. The unfinished journey of his father's life must have haunted Abram during his time in Harran.

Bible scholars believe that Terah's work with bronze brought him into contact with military leaders who would have used brass or copper in armor or weapons - even suggesting Terah may have been Chief Armorer, a position with royal protection. This honor would have made Abram a kind of prince among the Hittites.

But when Terah died in Harran, Abram did not stay at the forge or in his father's successful statuary shop, he set out as a traveling merchant-prince, involved in the risky but exciting caravan trade. However, throughout the Assyrian and Hittite Empires, tradesmen and merchants were strictly regulated.

THE LAW OF THE LAND

We actually know a good deal about how business operated at the time of Abraham because so many legal and business documents survived. These clay cuneiform tablets age far better than papyrus. Thousands of years later, we can read how international business activities were regulated.

One particular tablet tells us how the two neighboring Hittite kings agreed to limit the time that merchants from the city of Ura can do business in the city of Ugarit. Ura's traveling merchants were only allowed access to Ugarit's markets during the summer months, after that, the merchants had to return to Ura.

Ura was a city famous for its "tamkârutum," or foreign trade, the occupation of the "tamkârum" or merchants.

The nature of tamkârum activities was built around families. Abram's family worked in the metal industry, but Abram did not settle for being a craftsman or a salesman, he wanted to be a producer, but in order to produce metals one needed land, either to build a forge independent of a temple complex, or one needed to own the actual mines where ore is extracted. This was nearly impossible at that time.

The two kings' regulatory agreement also prohibited any real estate sales in their respective lands to these traveling merchants. This prohibition was part of a longstanding practice to keep merchants on the move in order to prevent them from exploiting their theaters of operation or gaining enough wealth to fortify themselves and become military rivals of the kings.

The monarchies of the Middle East in the time of the Talmud (up to and including King Solomon's Israel) enjoyed monopolies across many economic sectors. The powerful warrior-kings of the Hittites, Elamites, Babylonians, Egyptians, Assyrians, and others, used their constellation of polytheistic temples to extract taxes from citizens - in some ways, temples had the function of national banks.

So the Patriarchs, like the merchants of Ura, traveled abroad to do business. Settling down in a foreign area of opportunity would have been wonderful to men like Abram who were regularly kept on the move. In Hebrew, the word for "merchant" means literally "one who turns hither and yon." Acquiring real estate in the land of their activity was a chronic wish of the merchants - a goal that was structurally denied to them.

Abraham lived most of his adult life as a tamkârum, constantly traveling from place to place. Thanks to these newly found cuneiform tablets, scholars now think that Abraham came from Ura of the Kaldi. Based on the descriptions of Abraham's wealth in later life, it seems as though his merchant tribe used donkeys for local trade and camels for long-distance trade along caravan trade routes.

THE MERCHANT PRINCE

Abraham comes from beyond the Euphrates, works his trade in Canaan, visits Egypt, deals with Hittites, makes treaties with Philistines, forms military alliances with Amorites, fights kings from as far off as Elam, marries an Egyptian...His contacts and freedom of movement reflect a sophisticated international order which made such a career and enterprise possible.

None of it would have been possible had Abram stayed in his father's shop.

The story of Abraham's extraordinary purchase of the Cave of the Patriarchs in Hebron from the Hittites constitutes the first "real estate" of Israel. In settling here, in this rural region of Southern Canaan, Abraham formed an alliance with two local Amorite clans - one which was nomadic and the other who worked in the Egyptian copper mines of Timna. These were the very mines which had been his father's dream.

Probably the proximity to Egypt made Southern Canaan into a sort of no-man's land where both the Egyptians and Hittites tolerated each other's commercial enterprise. In the great cities to the north, east, and south, the royal monopolists were able to regulate the activities of merchants with a firm hand. But in Canaan, merchants could have a freer hand but would have to provide for their own security.

Unlike his timid father Terah, Abraham braved the big move to ply his trade as far south as Palestine for the freedom of opportunity he thereby gained. At the same time he had to secure the interests of his household and of his kinsmen by maintaining his own militia and by forming alliances with local Amorite chieftains (Genesis 14:13-14, 24). Abraham's family enterprise would even grow to capture the means of copper production!

Around 3,200 years ago, the great empires around the Mediterranean and the Middle East suddenly imploded. During this Bronze Age Collapse, Troy burned, Phoenicia splintered, the Egyptians retreated from Canaan, abandoning the copper mines of Timna, shrinking back to the banks of the Nile. In this power-vacuum amid the arid wastes of southern Canaan, a new power arose because of the initiative taken by Patriarchs like Abraham.

The severe depression lasted long enough to be considered civilization's first Dark Age. But like any economic downturn, an enterprising business person will capitalize on temporarily undervalued assets and emerge from the recession stronger than ever. This is what happened with Abraham.

"God tested Abraham..." Genesis 22:1

The Timna mines were taken over by semi-nomadic tribes tied to Abraham's confederation. The mine workers, Midianites and Kenites who were already known throughout the Levant for their metalwork, set up their own mining operation at Timna that would soon dwarf the previous Egyptian industry.

One of the first things this new desert confederation did at Timna was smash the on-site temple of the god Hathor, the Egyptian protector of miners. Instead, the area's metal workers worshiped the Canaanite god of metallurgy, a local God named "Yahweh."

Unsurprisingly, Yahweh's appearance in the Bible is usually accompanied by volcanic-like phenomena. For example, when He descends upon Mt. Sinai to reveal the Torah to the Jews, the mountain erupts in fire, billowing clouds accompanied by earthquakes and thunderstorms, spewing lava and molten red metal like that produced in the smelting process (Exodus 19:16-19).

Egyptian texts tell us that the cult of Yahweh first emerged in the southern Levant. The Bible itself says explicitly that God "came from Teman [Timna]" (Habbakuk 3:3) and "marched out of Edom" (Judges 5:4-5) – all place names associated with the area surrounding the Negev Valley.

As the Bronze Age gave way to the Iron Age, this smelting god, worshiped by the semi-nomadic peoples all over the southern Levant, became the solitary national deity of just one of these nations, located on the hill where the Canaanite god El lived -- giving us the name Israel.

The Israelites thrived because they had diversified their enterprise enough to survive the diminishment of the value of copper as the Iron Age transformed society. By the ninth century BCE, when the mines at

Timna were played-out, Abraham's people had wisely used their wealth to build entire cities and forge a Nation with political treaties.

Abraham's entrepreneurial nature allowed him to achieve great success in business. His family trade started as a single shop in Ura, then grew to a plum government contract Harran, allowing Abraham to venture beyond simple retail.

He built his tamkârutum into an entire alliance of business families in southern Canaan, all of whom surrounded a vital copper mine where they captured the means of production. They managed the trade of this highly valuable commodity along international caravan routes that they controlled. Their capital and real estate holdings grew steadily until their group became accepted as a major power as legitimate as those far more ancient nations which surrounded them.

"Be strong and courageous." Deuteronomy 31:6

DAVID

Three thousand years ago civilization around the Mediterranean suffered an economic collapse that is known as the first Dark Age. What had once been a flourishing cosmopolitan world with international trade and growing literacy fell into isolationism and ignorance for several hundred years.

King David lived in this calamitous time and yet he rose to power and wealth while the ancient great powers around him like the Trojans, Phoenicians, and Hittites, were all destroyed.

The Philistines of the Bible were the desperate last remnants of the collapsing Minoan Civilization. Made up of the warrior class and their slaves, the Philistines abandoned the island of Crete for the mainland looking for natural resources to live off of.

They were one of the fabled "Sea Peoples" whose piracy and ravaging terrorized nations as far away as Egypt and Greece. It is thought that they drove the ancient Phoenicians completely out of the northern Levant where they had once thrived.

As a result of the collapse of international supply chains and the end of peaceful international trade, most nations splintered into autonomous city states – this is what happened to Israel. The only cities that survived the First Dark Age were those with large enough walls. At the time of David, Israel had become a scattered tribal society ruled by various judges. The cities had to fend for themselves against hunger and the perennially marauding Philistines.

A large contingent of the Philistines settled in the former lands of the Phoenicians on the coastal plain north of Israel, a land in present day Lebanon and Syria. From here they set out on raids of destruction and pillage every winter.

One day, the Philistine army parked themselves overlooking the edge of the verdant Valley of Elah, but they were met by the Army of Saul from the tribe of Benjamin who had gathered men from other tribes. Saul camped across the valley on the hill above the valley. For weeks, the two sat deadlocked.

Finally, the Philistines opted for single combat. They sent their mightiest warrior down into the valley floor, and he calls out: "Send your mightiest warrior down," hoping to settle the war, just the two of them.

We all know who the Philistines send: Goliath was 6 feet 9 inches tall. He was fully loaded with heavy bronze armor, he holds a giant sword and a javelin and a spear. He's so terrifying that naturally none of the Israelites want to fight him.

The only person who will come forward is a "shepherd boy." David was Saul's son-in-law and the youngest of the many men in Saul's household.

David makes his case to Saul for why he is fit for single combat against Goliath arguing that he had been defending his flock against lions and wolves for years. He hopes to prove his nerve, not his aim.

With no other option, likely very disappointed in the boy's naivete, Saul agrees to the youngster's plea, but he asks David to at least wear some armor. David insists against Saul's idea.

"And David girded his sword upon his apparel, and he assayed to go; for he had not proved it. And David said unto Saul, I cannot go with these; for I have not proved them. And David put them off him." 1 Samuel 17:39

David just puts a sword under his belt and drops Saul's heavy armor which he had never worn before – he had "not proved" it.

Instead, David reaches down on the ground and picks up five smooth stones. He puts them in his shepherd's bag and walks down the mountainside with his shepherd's staff to meet the giant.

Goliath sees this boy coming and says "Am I a dog that you would come to me with sticks?" Surely laughing at his own joke. David answers by taking one of the stones out of his pouch, he puts it in his sling and winds up the speed with which he lets loose a shot that hits the giant right between the eyes.

Goliath falls down either dead or unconscious, at least dazed, but quickly the shepherd boy runs over and takes his sword and cuts off Goliath's head. End of battle.

WELL-PRACTICED SKILLS

Here is what the insightful business person can take from this Bible story. David knew his weapon - he was never an underdog. David knows that his specific skill set has certain advantages against Goliath's style of fighting.

David's advantages were agility of movement and accuracy from a distance. He knew not to compromise those advantages, either with Saul's heavy armor or by getting into close-combat. A sword fight with a bigger swordsman would have been suicide.

David graciously rejects Saul's advice because he knew that if he kept to his plan and exploited Goliath's weakness, young David would win. David knew that in the rock-paper-scissors face-off of ancient warfare styles, he actually had the advantage.

Armies in those days were made up of three kinds of warriors: first was cavalry, men on horseback and armored chariots. There was heavy infantry like Goliath, these were heavily-armored foot soldiers with swords and shields. And then there's artillery, who are archers and slingers.

The sling is not a slingshot like a child's toy. The sling is an incredibly devastating weapon. When David winds up the speed of his leather pouch with a stone inside, the sling's long strings hum loudly.

As the slinger lets go of one of the two strings connected to his pouch, the rock is spinning at seven revolutions per second. A longer sling line means that when the rock is released, it travels at around 38 yards-per-second or more than 77 miles-per-hour. Calculations on the ballistics reveal that the stopping power of the rock fired from David's sling was likely equal to the stopping power of a .38 caliber handgun.

The Bible specifically tells us that David took the time to find five smooth stones. The smoother the stone, the less chance of having a snag on the fabric of the sling's pouch upon release – a smooth stone is easiest to aim.

Experienced slingers could hit targets at distances of up to 200 yards. We know that slingers in ancient times were capable of hitting birds in flight. When David lines up opposite Goliath, he is close enough for the two to talk with each other. David has every expectation of hitting Goliath's face, directly in the eye gap of Goliath's giant helmet.

THINKING OUTSIDE THE BOX

Goliath and the Philistines expected that the Israelites would send down another heavy infantryman to fight in an equal duel. But the rules of the engagement were not specified. Goliath even said, after calling for a challenger and getting no response, "Is there not ANYONE who will fight me?"

We can tell from the way Saul reacted to David volunteering that he also had the same expectation – that David was volunteering for hand-to-hand combat against a Heavy Infantryman. This is why Saul tries to load David up with infantry armor.

But David recognized his advantage and took the opportunity when Goliath said "anyone."

When Goliath says, "Come to me that I might feed your flesh to the birds of the heavens and the beasts of the field," the phrase "come to me" is a hint of Goliath's vulnerability. No way would David make anything easy for his opponent. He keeps his distance which is where the slinger excels.

What is usually missing in stories of David vs Goliath is the lesson of strategic intelligence on display. This wasn't a case of an underdog winning because of a miracle. This came about because of practice.

The fact is that giants are not as strong and powerful as they want us to believe. Not only are they incapable of nimble quick movement like a slinger, but they might not even be able to move forward at all.

The same thing is true of monopolies and mega-corporations today. Sometimes a small business, "the shepherd boy," is actually an expert slinger who found five smooth stones. We each need to know our skill and hone it. We need to look for strategic opportunities to apply the skill. And, additionally in business, we need to be brave.

The boy who would become King David went on to apply this lesson to his nationhood. Surrounded by giant empires like Egypt and Assyria, Israel remains nimble and strategic.

When they do battle, they strike quickly and then offer favorable peace terms. David went to all of the other nearby states that had been terrorized yearly by the Philistines: the peoples of Edom, Moab, Ammon, Amalek, Damascus. He either collected taxes to not attack or he attacked once and then offered to never do it again.

Extracting yearly tax payments from its neighbors made Israel a very wealthy nation in David's time.

SOLOMON

Solomon is perhaps the Biblical figure who is most readily connected to riches and wealth. According to 2 Chronicles 9:20, he possessed so much gold that silver's worth was diminished. People are still searching for his secret treasures today because of his outrageous fortune.

In his own time, he was one of the five richest men alive. But he is also known for his wisdom. King Solomon wrote:

"The words of the wise are like goads, their collected sayings are like a nail-studded stick with which a shepherd drives the sheep. The words of the wise prod us to live well. They're like nails hammered home, holding life together. They are given by God, the one Shepherd. Ecclesiastes 12:11

King Solomon, the third leader of the Jewish Kingdom, is often portrayed as a paragon of wisdom, famed throughout his kingdom for his sage judgment. People traveled far and wide to seek his counsel. His most glorified moments occur early in his reign. The reason for this contains insights valuable to any business person.

THE PRIMACY OF WISDOM

When Solomon became King, he was a young man of about eighteen years old. He had big shoes to fill as David's successor. Solomon was not yet filled with his famous wisdom when he first ascended to the throne. When he first ascended the throne, his main trait was that he was earnest.

Like so many of us, his good thing was also his bad thing: Earnestness can be a strength because it makes you pure of heart, focused on your convictions, dedicated; but earnestness can easily slide into the kind of naiveté that unscrupulous neighbors will always seek to exploit.

Hoping for the seasoning that usually comes with age and experience, Solomon took a work retreat before really settling into his job as King. This pre-startup retreat is a practice many founders still do today - it can be as simple as a weekend away from the office, somewhere conducive to clear thought and contemplation. Go armed with a workshop guide to facilitate "Finding Your Purpose." This particular workshop is a highly recommended annual reflection for recent graduates, early career, and mid-career professionals.

Solomon's work retreat took the form of a pilgrimage to Mount Gibeon, where the tabernacle of Moses was located. He was to offer a thousand burnt offerings to the Lord. He asked God not for riches. Neither did he ask to be honored by all men. Instead, Solomon asked God:

Give me wisdom and knowledge, that I may go out and come in before this people; for who can judge this great people of Yours?
2 Chronicles 1:10

Another account in the Book of 1 Kings tells us that Solomon asked the Lord, "Therefore give to Your servant an understanding heart to judge Your people, that I may discern between good and evil. For who is able to judge this great people of Yours?"

When Solomon asked for wisdom and knowledge he was asking for an understanding heart. The word "understanding" here is the Hebrew word *shama*, which means "to hear intelligently." The Bible records that Solomon's request pleased the Lord (1 Kings 3:10).

The job of Solomon as judge was the task that clearly worried the teenager the most. How could he pass judgment over his elders, adjudicate between successful rivals in a public court?

He needed to be able to truly hear his petitioners and with his intelligence discern the truth.

Solomon only asked for wisdom but the Lord added "riches and wealth and honor" in what was given to Solomon because of how he approached his work.

This means that knowledge is more valuable than other currencies. A currency is any "stuff" that gets work done, or "thing" which makes business possible. The story of Solomon reiterates to a business person that the four currencies are, in this order:

1. Knowledge
2. People
3. Time
4. Money

Actual cash is the least important kind of currency. Knowledge and wisdom is the most important kind of currency. Solomon could have asked God for any sort of blessing, including wealth or good health. However, Solomon chose wisdom.

For us to pursue Knowledge we must be disciplined, paying careful attention to the choices we make as we build and operate our business. We must evaluate our decisions, listening for truth. We must strive to keep our own thoughts and plans oriented towards truth. The Bible urges us to remember:

"Finally, brothers and sisters, whatever is true, whatever is noble, whatever is right, whatever is pure, whatever is lovely, whatever is admirable – if anything is excellent or praiseworthy – think about such things." Philippians 4:8

In other words, learn from what works. Try new approaches and carefully chart the results. Refine your practices and learn from everything, listening closely with an understanding heart.

God was pleased with Solomon's choice to pursue wisdom over other pursuits because armed with this, Solomon would be able to get every other kind of currency.

Also, Solomon's initial humility about the heavy responsibilities before him pleased God. We can make that same choice ourselves. We must pursue knowledge first.

We must remain humble as a student and also stay humble in later life. This is the primacy of knowledge in business and the cautionary tale of Solomon's later years.

WISE REASONING

Solomon's downfall also contains lessons. Rather than retaining his humility later in life, his profligacy and extravagance eventually led to the downfall of his dynasty.

"Now King Solomon loved many foreign women along with the daughter of Pharaoh: Moabite, Ammonite, Edomite, Sidonian, and Hittite women, from the nations concerning which the Lord had said to the sons of Israel, 'You shall not associate with them, nor shall they associate with you, for they will surely turn your heart away after their gods.' Solomon held fast to these in love. He had <u>seven hundred</u> wives, princesses, and three hundred concubines, and his wives turned his heart away. For when Solomon was old, his wives turned his heart away after other gods; and his heart was not wholly devoted to the Lord his God, as the heart of David his father had been." 1 Kings 11:1-4

Solomon's wives included Princesses - these marriages constituted business mergers of his nation to others. Solomon was directed to stay focused on the fate of his nation but instead he went and partnered with too many rivals and neighbors.

This would be like a businessman taking on 700 business partners. This was his error. The women themselves were not evil, but their own nations' interests did dilute the strength of Solomon's Israel.

Why did King Solomon's wisdom fail to guide him in controlling his own life? This wise man was famous for adjudicating over others but when it came to the most important decisions in his own life, Solomon lacked insight. This contributed greatly to his kingdom's demise. This phenomenon is today known in the field of Psychology as Solomon's Paradox.

One reason for this phenomenon is that people tend to adopt the first-person perspective when faced with their personal problems and the third-person perspective when thinking about others' issues.

When making choices about career prospects and anticipating market forces, people who reasoned from an ego-decentering perspective perform better than those who immerse their own perspectives upon the facts.

Later in life, when Solomon was far removed from being the humble boy who asked God for wisdom, his long reign in his luxurious palace with so many alliances at cross-purposes made his own experiences unsuitable for a model upon which to rightly see the facts of his own life. He had lost context.

Essentially: some people are wiser when reflecting on other people's problems compared with their own. This is a problem that comes with ego and pride. Self-distancing helps eliminate this asymmetry in our reasoning.

People who recognize the limits of their knowledge and the importance of compromise and future change, and who consider other people's perspectives, have better reasoning outcomes. People who try to filter every decision through the lens of their own experience have worse outcomes.

BUILD THE TEMPLE

Solomon's marriage to the daughter of Pharaoh came with a significant dowry. His nation would enjoy tight connections with the major power of the time. With the money, Solomon could pursue building Solomon's Temple. This was the most important building project for his entire nation.

The project had a promising start but several complications arose that indicate an internal conflict within Solomon. The King completes the work on the temple structure in seven years (1 Kings 6:38), but the temple is not furnished inside and therefore it is not suitable for worship until much later (Kings 7:51). In the meantime, Solomon completes work on his own palace complex as well as the separate palace for his Egyptian wife (Kings 7:8).

This delay in the temple's completion would have presented a large dilemma for the people since it would have meant that they were forced to continue worship in the mountain caves like those on Gibeon while the temple sat empty in Jerusalem. We are told Solomon dedicated thirteen years to the work of his own house, versus the seven years required for the building of the temple for all of Israel. (Kings 6:38-7:1)

After this poorly project-managed building program, Solomon consecrates the temple for worship and receives a vision from the Lord in which God warns him of the dangers of a divided heart - which are like the dangers of a muddied business plan or poor project management. Solomon did not take the warning. All business people today must take this project management warning.

DON'T SPLIT THE BABY

As Biblical lore goes, King Solomon once solved a maternity dispute between two women who each claimed a child as her own. Solomon ruled that they would cut the baby in half and divide it between the two women, knowing the child's real mother would gladly forfeit her claim rather than see her child lose its life.

Applied to business: If you're considering divestiture of a product or business division, consider whether that kind of sale is your only option. Does it make sense to investigate selling minority or majority stakes of your whole company with the right buyer?

In this scenario, you may get a higher value and then even get a second bite of the apple down the road. Additionally, do not dilute your brand.

"Fear of the Lord is the beginning of wisdom."
Psalms 111:10

JOB

One day, Satan presents God a challenge, a debate; "would a wealthy, righteous man remain righteous if he lost his money or would he fall from righteousness?

God picks his man. Job of Utz is everything that God wants a businessman to be. We should model ourselves as righteous business people on Job. And we should learn from what he says about wicked business people to guard against what we should not become.

We learn that Job has seven sons and three daughters. He owns 7,000 sheep, 3,000 camels, 500 hundred yoke of cattle, and 500 she-donkeys. He owns property and has many workers. He is quite similar in lifestyle to a large corporate CEO.

One day, tragedy strikes Job and all of his children die, he loses all his possessions. His wife watches helplessly as his body is covered with boils.

As Job attempts to understand the reasons for his tragedies the reader learns many important lessons about the meaning of life and how people should live their lives in business.

In one view, The Book of Job is the story of a man who loses everything despite his good deeds, and attempts to answer the classic conundrum of "why bad things happen to good people."

But seen another way, The Book of Job is a blueprint for righteous business practices.

Like many people today, Job's three friends – Eliphaz the Temanite, Bildad the Shuhite, and Zophar the Naamathite – are of the opinion that God only punishes those who are not righteous. This is nonsense, as we know.

In the story, Job gets the chance to defend himself to his friends and neighbors. He proves himself righteous - as God knew he was, and as his own friends knew too. What does Job do? He first differentiates himself from wicked businessmen:

"They [wicked bosses] drive away the orphan's donkey and take the widow's ox in pledge. They thrust the needy from the path and force all the poor of the land into hiding. Like wild donkeys in the desert, the poor go about their labor of foraging food; the wasteland provides food for their children. They [the laborers of the wicked] harvest the wheat fields and glean in the vineyards of the wicked. Lacking clothes, they spend the night naked; they have nothing to cover themselves in the cold. They are drenched by mountain rains and hug the rocks for lack of shelter. The fatherless child is snatched from the breast; the infant of the poor is seized for a debt. Lacking clothes, they go about naked; they carry the sheaves of wheat, but still go hungry. They crush olives among the terraces; they tread the winepresses, yet suffer thirst. The groans of the people rise from the city, and the souls of the wounded cry out for help. But God charges no one with wrongdoing." Job 24: 1-12.

Job describes the vicious ways that the wicked businessmen harm the underclass. Key among the misdeeds of wicked businessmen is how they mistreat laborers.

These poor laborers have to work at night unclothed and are constantly hungry. Job, of course, does not treat his laborers in such a manner. Job blames wicked businessmen for poverty and homelessness.

This is probably the most important lesson of Job: a business owner is obligated to help the needy and be especially concerned with the welfare of laborers.

Job rages that God does not help the groans of the people whose suffering is due to vile businessmen who are allowed to remain rich despite being so wicked.

In Chapter 34, Elihu, another one of the people who have come to hear Job complain about God's inhumanity to man, suggests that God does hear the cry of the needy. He says God expects humans to band together to create a just legal system and use it to eradicate evil.

In the words of Elihu:

"People will unite in the face of oppression, and they will cry out to be rescued from the oppressors' strong hand" Job 35:9.

Job accepts that God punishes those who ignore the plight of the disadvantaged, but he has not been guilty of this offense. Job helps the disadvantaged.

Job says that a good businessman will not force his employees to live below the poverty line. Job agrees that a good businessman will build just systems for addressing grievances and alleviating worker suffering.

In the world of business today, this might be a quarterly review system that includes anonymous feedback for management. It could be a good relationship with the labor leaders that work with the owner, but there needs to be a system of economic justice that all sides support.

Job knows that what he has done with this workforce is exemplary. Job cares. Not only did Job take care of the poor and needy and concern himself with the welfare of his employees, but evidently, victims of wicked oppressors come to Job asking that he go investigate their claims of injustice.

Job was a friend to the laborer and he stood against wicked businessmen. Injustices against the weaker members of society were of great concern to Job and he helped other workers deal with wrongs. This is why God loved him.

Many wealthy people treat servants as possessions and show them no respect but Job regarded his servants as his equals since God made everyone.

His neighbors all knew that Job was a beloved civic leader.

"I was a father to the needy; and the cause of him that I knew not, I would investigate." Job 29:16.

Job recognized that it was morally wrong to exploit any human being because everyone — master and servant – was created by God. This is why Job was careful not to abuse the rights of his male or female servants. What Job says about his day and age could be said about some selfish CEOs today whose great profits are due to exploiting underpaid workers.

By any standard, Job would be considered a community leader. He is wealthy and yet he is trusted by the working class as their champion. When he enters the public square, high-ranking citizens listen to his opinions. They allow him to rail against God because it truly seems that his anger at God is justified.

Finally, God steps in and stops Job from the whirlwind, putting the mortal in his place. "Where were you when I laid the foundations of the Earth? Tell me, if you know so much." And He says:

"Here your proud waves must stop!" Job 38:4-11

In other words, there are bigger designs at play that are far beyond the control of even the richest person on Earth. The world is a massive system of complex systems that no single person can grasp. God goes on to humble Job by listing all of the other animals that God controls.

God says the world is full of marvelous wild creatures who accomplish amazing feats without any human help or human understanding.

At last, Job drops his defenses and realizes his lack of control over creation and his insignificance in the universe. He repents his former arrogance and ignorance.

Job knew the responsibilities of wealthy people but needed to understand the limitations of powerful people:

"Relax your grip on your money and abandon your gold-plated luxury." Job 22:24

It took a lot of suffering to get Job's attention. Similarly, many business owners are finally awakening to the fragility of our supply chain issues in an international marketplace and only now finally understanding the planet's fragility and the interconnected fate of all our human societies in the face of climate change.

The Job story admonishes all of us who are leaders, or would-be leaders to pay attention, to be humble about our own ability to control outcomes, and to harmonize our actions with natural systems.

In the end, Job's wealth is returned to him twofold. He ended up twice as rich as he was before. But more importantly, he is given new children and one of his first acts is to treat his daughters as equal to his sons - he declares that they too will receive a share of inheritance! This act of feminism was eons ahead of its time.

The thing to take from this coda of Job's tale is that for as great a businessman as he was before his calamities, for how much he cared about ending homelessness and fighting on behalf of exploited workers, even standing against wicked businessmen, Job emerges from bankruptcy an even better person.

In treating women as equal to men Job ends up twice as righteous as he was before all his calamities.

JOSEPH

The life story of Joseph (he of the coat) teaches key business lessons that apply to today. Joseph's entrepreneurial characteristics can be folded into a life story that should be helpful to many of us who have changed careers several times.

If you worry that your "varied" resume makes you look like you lack focus, you could always position yourself as a worker in the model of the great Joseph of the Bible.

Being the youngest and favorite son, Joseph's father instructs him to go be an overseer of his older siblings at work in the fields. Joseph served as a kind of foreman, sharing intel with his father about what the other sons were up to. This clearly did not go over well with his brothers.

Joseph had no idea why his siblings were so deceptive and scheming and jealous, but it turned out that this exact behavior was present in his family's DNA. When his father Jacob was a young man, he and his mother schemed so that Jacob would get the blessing which belonged to his own twin brother Esau.

One generation later, the same behavior presents itself in Jacob's sons. Through no fault of his own, Joseph fell victim to an emotion-regulation issue inherent in his family.

Joseph did not know this secret about his father's past so he had no reason to suspect this behavior of his brothers. One lesson to take from this is the value of anticipation: In business, if you can anticipate the behavior of someone else, then you will have a better chance of including them in your plans. If you cannot anticipate their behavior, any plan of yours that includes them, in any way, becomes more risky.

The first career section of Joseph's life closes when his resentful siblings decide he is spoiled and a snitch. We are told they are "jealous" of his favor with their father. As a result, Joseph was sold into slavery by his older siblings. He is sent off to an Egyptian named Potiphar.

What's notable about this huge change in Joseph's fortunes is that Joseph's family business was raising cattle, but in Egypt, Joseph finds himself in a foreign land doing domestic work that was extremely different from anything he had done before. A large career change, indeed.

HOUSE SLAVE

It turns out that the reason his father had trusted him to be an overseer of his more senior workers was because Joseph was indeed a diligent worker. We can see this because, quickly, his new Egyptian bosses recognize that Joseph is a good worker and trustworthy manager. Joseph rises in the ranks among the house servants.

It may not look on paper like Joseph was a dedicated worker because he had only worked on his father's ranch for a short period of time, and now here he was doing something completely different.

But sometimes the kind of professional we are capable of being is not reflected on our paper resume. Sometimes our resume can even tell the opposite story of our true potential.

Consider Joseph's career in Egypt. Before long, Joseph found himself in charge of Potiphar's house. Potiphar was the Chief of the Pharaoh's Guard.

Joseph found himself in charge of a staff, he had to manage budgets, he probably had to interact with guests from the Pharaoh's court or other military leaders. Joseph certainly had to meet with and debrief the masters of the house on a regular basis.

It is a job with enormous responsibilities to be anything like a Chief of Staff. This kind of job takes incredible project management skill and soft skills and by all accounts, Joseph excelled.

We are told that Joseph was always focused on doing right by his boss and increasing his wealth in business:

"From the time he put him in charge of his household and of all that he owned, the Lord blessed the household of the Egyptian because of Joseph." Genesis 39:5

Joseph had the ability to help others prosper. This is a great gift; the ability to see gaps and know how to fill them - or find a way to get them filled - is exactly the kind of talent that a good boss promotes into a foreman.

It is precisely the skill set that a military leader would promote into a Chief of Staff position. We can assume that this was Joseph's great talent. He had to know he was talented in this way. First Jacob recognized it, now Potiphar - this was Joseph's great working skill.

What did he do with his skill? What could he do? Circumstances beyond his control had put him in this situation far from home, in a less than ideal situation, but Joseph was focused on helping Potiphar.

Potiphar's entire household, including the field, prospered because of Joseph. Joseph's success as a worker is measurable by how much effort and resources he dedicated to the success and prosperity of others. These are lessons we should take whenever we are employees, even doing the kinds of work that is new or less appealing than we are used to.

PRISON ASSISTANT

Joseph's next stint was in an Egyptian prison. There he distinguished himself with excellent work and was made leader, helping the Warden and Guards provide for the prisoners.

While doing his work, he met two of the Pharaoh's officials who had dreams they could not understand. This was a talent of Joseph's too. It had never been his full-time job, this prognostication, but Joseph dabbled. Joseph offered his services to help the officials while they were visiting the Warden. The court officials gave Joseph a chance because of his high status at the prison.

Joseph interpreted the dreams for the two royal court officials with enough specificity that the members of the court remembered him well. As time went on at the Pharaoh's palace, it turned out that Joseph's interpretations were correct and the events of the dreamers' lives unfolded as Joseph had explained they would.

Years later, the Pharaoh had a dream that he found confusing and troubling. The members of court who had met Joseph by chance remembered him years later. They recommended that the prison's cupbearer be brought to the palace.

The reason was simple. Joseph was doing one of the most important things a business person who wishes to get ahead should do:

Be smart…on purpose…in public.

One need not tirelessly self-promote, doling out business cards to everyone you meet. If you have a skill, it is best if someone else is the one to say that you have a talent. Always let somebody else call you a genius. An endorsement from a trusted intermediary is the best promotion any business can receive. Joseph had a genius for dream interpretation, but he wasn't insufferable about pitching himself to random customers.

He was smart on purpose in public -- and the work found him.

PHARAOH'S ADVISOR

When he is brought to the Pharaoh, Joseph listens to the dream. The dream had been vexing the Pharaoh for a few reasons which give us some psychological insight not only into the state of the Egyptian monarchy of the time, but also into Joseph's ability to read a room and work power wisely.

A man as powerful as Pharaoh is considered by those around him to be god-like. The Pharaoh lives in a world of black-and-white. If he wanted someone to die, they were killed immediately. His power was frightening. Whether or not he believed that he was all-knowing doesn't change the fact that for him to face something as mysterious as a nebulous dream must have been unnerving.

That the mystery was coming from inside the Pharaoh's own mind must have made the problem twice as vexing. It's not like he could have the messenger executed and be rid of the message. The problem is inside his own unconscious mind.

Joseph's interpretation declares that the dream is about an upcoming famine.

"Seven years of great abundance are coming throughout the land of Egypt, but seven years of famine will follow them."
Genesis 41:29-30

This interpretation does something great. It flips the mystery into a hypothetical. Joseph guides the Pharaoh from an unknown unknown into just a mere *known* unknown: There will be a famine in the near future. Exactly when is unknown, but *what* is certain -- famine.

When did the years of abundance begin exactly? Everyone would know that was hard to pin down. Was all this a ruse by Joseph? Famines are cyclical. Any worker like Joseph who had come from working outdoors knows this.

Cleverly, Joseph turns the known element of time into an opportunity that plays into the Pharaoh's strengths as a builder and as the chief executive of a massive administrative state. What Joseph does is prove himself to be a creative problem solver.

In business, all problems can be solved with money and time. If you are short on time, solving the problem will take more money. If you are short on money, it will take more time. By defining the problem as a famine, what Joseph presents is a new factor: they have a limited amount of time to solve the problem…A problem which Joseph has redefined. Because he understands the new problem, he also presents his solution.

This is similar to a famous story from the world of business in the 1920s. Bad breath wasn't thought of as a medical condition until the Listerine company realized that it could help them sell mouthwash. The owner of Listerine and his son invented the word "Halitosis." They defined Halitosis as a disorder that makes you unpopular. Advertisements informing the public about the danger of Halitosis also introduced the product that would solve the problem…a problem that they defined.

Because now the Pharaoh had a defined problem that he could flex his muscles on, implementing Joseph's solution to the problem became the most pressing project in Egypt for the next several years.

For these years, Joseph lived in the luxurious palace working on his solution. His solution was a collection of ideas which amount to good business: Firstly, save during the years of great abundance.

"Take a fifth of the harvest," Genesis 41:34

Joseph means for Egypt to save 20% of all income and put it away like in a Social Security lockbox. Joseph's idea was so elegant and wide-ranging that he was appointed second in power only to Pharaoh himself in order to make sure that the solution was to Joseph's "dream interpretation" standards. Joseph must have interfaced with every sector of the economy to build up Egypt's reserves.

The other innovation that Joseph introduced was to decentralize some of Egypt's enormous administrative state.

"They should collect all the food of these good years that are coming and store up…to be kept in the cities for food."
Genesis 41:35

Many storehouses were built in many different cities to store the food. This would cut down on spoilage and cut down on transportation headaches when it came time to distribute the reserved food supply.

Joseph also thought deeply into the user stories of his project. What would people do when the famine struck? When a farmer has no grain to make money what will he do if he needs money?

Joseph knew that farmers and ranchers like his father, those who would be hardest hit by a famine, would have only one physical asset: Livestock.

Joseph suggested that the Pharaoh accept livestock and land as currency from those who had no cash when the time of famine came.

This policy change would have helped people like his father survive. This innovation became a permanent change in the Egyptian system of land tenure. Because of this idea, during hard times, small farm owners became tenants on ever-expanding royal lands of the Pharaoh.

Whenever Joseph worked for someone, he fought for them to succeed. Joseph's idea led to the Egyptian dynasty becoming the largest manager of land in the Empire by far. Every time there was an economic downturn, the Pharaoh was the only one who would come out ahead.

This was admittedly shortsighted on the part of the Pharaoh.

The secondary consequence to this idea of enriching the richest 1% would be a growing sense of resentment amongst the tenant class who lived and worked under rentier serfdom for generations while the strength of the Egyptian administrative state only grew in size.

This exact tension would eventually boil over with a populist uprising which is documented in the story of Moses. However, that is not so much a business lesson as a political lesson for a different day.

CORNELIUS THE CENTURION

In the book of Acts 10:1-48, we hear the story of Cornelius. This story also is full of business lessons.

"There was a certain man in Caesarea called Cornelius, a centurion of what was called the Italian Regiment, a devout man and one who feared God with all his household, who gave alms generously to the people, and prayed to God always." Acts 10:1

Cornelius was a rich Gentile from Italy who, like many other superstitious Roman soldiers stationed in faraway lands, took up the practice of praying to the local gods. For the years that Cornelius was living in the Levant serving with his regiment, Cornelius prayed to local God Yahweh, the God of the Jews.

It is stressed repeatedly in The Book of Acts that Cornelius gave generously to the poor. Cornelius heard that Peter, a leader of a new sect of Jews was in his town - the Book of Acts attributes this rumor mill to the Holy Spirit. Notably, Cornelius sends three messengers to follow Peter to Joppa with an invitation to come back and visit him at his estate.

Peter accepted Cornelius's invitation for a religious discussion in the Roman's home. The three servants who Cornelius had dispatched to retrieve Peter conveyed their master's interest in the message that Peter was preaching.

Cornelius was not exactly the kind of customer Peter had been focusing on. But the opportunity was rich. However, in order to land this potential client, Peter had to shed some of his outdated business practices; In those days, an observant Jew was supposed to follow the high court's edict of religious discrimination and separate foods and people into the categories of clean and unclean. Peter would have to break this rule, go into the home of an unclean person and eat his non-kosher food.

"And the following day they entered Caesarea. Now Cornelius was waiting for them, and had called together his relatives and close friends. As Peter was coming in, Cornelius met him and fell down at his feet and worshiped him. But Peter lifted him up, saying, "Stand up; I myself am also a man." Acts 10:24

Peter's humility in this moment with the wealthy Cornelius is notable. The status difference between the two men was unmistakable: Peter was poor, he had been traveling for years with one assistant, homeless - subsisting on charity. As soon as Peter entered the well-appointed home, he established an equality between himself and the rich Roman.

Peter saw the value in ending the practice of religious discrimination with a humility that matched the graciousness of his polite host. Matching that spirit of generosity, Cornelius asked Peter to preach his message.

Cornelius listens while Peter tells him about Jesus and his call for peace love, and at the end of Peter's story, the two conclude that God wants them to see each other as equals in a new way, as friends in a new fellowship. Peter's missional methods were strategic, not xenophobic. He was expanding his market, he was pushing his product into new sectors. These are excellent sales practices.

Peter's good salesmanship aside, what did Cornelius do that we can take business lessons from?

HUMILITY DEFEATS ARROGANCE

Consider Cornelius' posture. Cornelius the Centurion commanded 100 soldiers, owned many slaves, owned land, and was clearly a man of wealth. But it was his humility and curiosity that led him to achieve even greater success as a leader of his fellow gentile converts. Humility and curiosity are qualities that surely contributed to his wealth in the first place, qualities which should not be discounted as pre-existing conditions.

Most tellingly, Cornelius appears to have been a lifelong learner. Cornelius likely grew up with religious lessons in the rites and rituals of the panoply of Roman gods like Jupiter, Juno, Minerva, and Mars. But throughout his travels, his open mind led him to learn of new gods, and learn how to adapt to the local ways.

With the Judeans, Cornelius adopted Judaism. Cornelius remained so open-minded that even as a comfortable practitioner of Judaism, he was interested in this splinter group of outcast Jews - the followers of Jesus.

The Cornelius this presents to us is the kind of enterprising person who gains success upon success and who does not let their past success go to waste or wither away by idle passivity. Cornelius did not rest on the laurels of his wealth, nor did he content himself with his successful status quo. He inquired with outsiders who had new information, he took meetings with them, and did so with the humility of an eager student.

As an observant Jew, Cornelius had to have been told that the zealot preachers and the dangerous Nazarenes like Peter were out of favor with the Pharisees, Sanhedrin, and temple elites. Some of Peter's Deacons were even executed for heresy. Cornelius ignored this discrimination and potential social stigma.

In business, we must be like Cornelius, willing to take meetings with people who some might shun as beneath us. We must be open to new opportunities, new ideas. We must adapt and learn.

It is a harder path to take, surely, but sometimes a person like Peter will walk into our office and change the world with us.

LYDIA

Paul the Apostle wanted to evangelize on the southern coast of The Black Sea. But one night on his way there, he dreamed that a Macedonian was begging for him to come to his aid. Paul recognized that this divine design overruled his plan. Immediately, Paul and his three companions, Luke, Timothy, and Silas set out on a ship from the Anatolian port of Troas bound for Greece.

After passing through the island of Samothrace, the Apostles finally reached Philippi, the principal city in that stretch of Macedonia. (Acts 16:6-12).

Though Philippi had been founded by Greeks in 360 BC, by King Philip II of Macedonia (the father of Alexander the Great), Philippi had been a Roman colony for the last 70 years.

But having once been the royal seat of the throne of Macedonia, there was still much aristocratic luster about Philippi. This glamor drew both wealthy individuals and merchants who deal in luxury items. That Alexander the Great started his conquest of the known world from this town also left a long shadow.

The Apostles began to preach about another conqueror of the universe, who would liberate the world...without a sword. One day, they spoke with women gathered on the shore of the Gangites River. Among them was a woman who listened attentively and immediately asked to be baptized with her whole family (Acts 16:14-15). This was Lydia.

The Bible tells us she was a wealthy businesswoman - a manufacturer and seller of purple dyes and fabrics for which her home city of Thyatira was famous.

It is striking that Lydia did not keep the joy of her conversion to herself, but wanted to win those closest to her too. An adroit businesswoman is prudent and thoughtful. She knows how to examine everything carefully. In this case, however, she did not hesitate or reflect for an instant. With stunning alacrity, she decided to receive baptism.

The Apostles must have been amazed to witness a resolute and firm business woman like Lydia, gifted with an overseer's commanding voice and accustomed to exercising authority, as she led all the servants of her house and business to baptism as a follower of Jesus, the Nazarene. She then invites Paul, Luke, Timothy, and Silas to stay at her estate.

It was not Paul's custom to accept donations too easily (2 Corinthians 11:9; 1 Thessalonians 2:9; 2 Thes 3:8), which could make him the target of slander, suggesting that he "evangelized" for profit. Paul regularly objected to such offers. Nevertheless, as the Bible tells us, Lydia "prevailed upon" them to accept her offer, thus manifesting her remarkable personality and strength of will. She would not take no for an answer.

After Paul baptized Lydia as the very first Christian convert in Europe, she said something very important to Paul:

"If you have judged me to be faithful to the Lord, come to my house and stay" Acts 16:15.

This question reveals her business genius: Reframing the ask.

There is a prudence to how she insisted upon getting her way with the Apostles. With humility and wisdom, she persuaded them by converting Paul's decision away from whether or not they should accept her invitation, and turned it instead onto a question of whether or not their conversion of her was true and fruitful - in other words, successful. The Apostle had to answer in the affirmative!

It is a brilliant reframing of any sales pitch which turns the buyer into the seller.

LYDIA SUPER-CONNECTOR

Luckily for the Apostles, Lydia was a remarkable woman. Being a foreigner to Philippi, she had probably become simply known as "Lydia" as in 'the woman from Lydia.'

For a long time, her hometown of Thyatira had been noted for the purple goods trade. This pigment was, without doubt, the costliest ink in ancient times. To make one gram of purple dye, ten thousand mollusks from a specific species had to be gathered from the coasts of the Mediterranean Sea and worked. The glands of these mollusks secreted a white fluid which gradually took on a purple color when exposed to sunlight.

For this reason, only emperors, kings and high-ranking dignitaries wore garments with purple dye, making them a luxury product. Selling specialty garments to royals and the richest people in Macedonia (at any price she wanted to set) had made Lydia very wealthy. The color purple was so rare that it was not until the 1850s with the invention of synthetic dyes, that the color was no longer a status symbol of obscene wealth.

According to the Bible, this purple dye trade was her personal business. Whether she built it on her own, inherited it from a deceased husband or a father without sons is unknown, either way Lydia ran it herself.

Lydia of Philippi had a unique standing in her time and place, both as a woman and as a merchant. As with many skills, the secrets of making royal purple were closely guarded, this knowledge was power. Power is attractive to others.

Being a merchant in a luxury trade granted her esteem in the community and entrée into the region's elite circles. Lydia must have known the social intricacies of the wealthy along with the technical details of her craft.

That she brought her family and employees along with her to also be baptized shows the kind of networker she was. She was likely what is known today as a super-connector. A person whose social network is large and varied with strong bonds. Paul's sales strategy of converting super connectors like Lydia was divinely inspired.

Winning support from Lydia was a massive victory for Paul and the hopes for the Church in Roman Europe. From that day on, Lydia's mansion would be the resting place for the missionaries and the community where the Christians of the region would gather for the celebration of the holy mysteries. In this way, Lydia's home became the first church in Europe.

After Paul's departure, Lydia and her congregation remained united in spirit. So much so that, later, when they learned of the trouble Paul was having elsewhere in a Macedonian jail cell, they sent him all that was necessary to help him survive and win release (Philippians 4:16-18). It would not be surprising if many of these gifts and political favors came from Lydia herself.

REFRAMING THE ASK

The greatest lesson to take from Lydia of Philippi was the skill with which she reframed an objection to her pitch. One of the most important things anyone in sales has to learn is that an objection to a sales pitch is not the same as a rejection.

One should see an objection as a worry - a concern that the buyer harbors and which the saleswoman has to address.

The Bible tells us that Lydia listened attentively to Paul's sermon. Good salesmanship requires listening to the buyer, hearing their concerns, and then, if there is an objection, reframing the conversation in a way that helps them understand why your product or service will create value for them. The objection itself is not a roadblock, rather, it is a road sign that helps the salesperson do her job.

When a salesperson hears a sales objection, you shouldn't scramble for a way to argue the fact. You should not try to change their mind. Instead, you should be prepared to address the (often withheld) worry in a way that helps change the buyer's perspective on the issue. The only way to do this is by having listened closely to what the buyer has said.

Being a manufacturer and saleswoman of a luxury item that was so costly that it had literally started wars, Lydia was likely well-practiced in one of the classic sales pitch reframing techniques which has to do with "cost vs value."

Some of the most common objections that salespeople will hear relate to price or budget. Buyers think a complaint about price is an easy escape hatch to get out of a sales conversation or to stall a pitch in its tracks.

The buyer who wants to say "no" believes that if something is too expensive, then it's simply too expensive--end of pitch. But a smart and experienced saleswoman like Lydia knows that's not the end.

In reality, price and budget objections are rarely absolute. As long as the return on the purchase justifies the cost, then buying can be presented as smart business. Buying becomes an investment. This reframing is shifting perspective from cost to value.

Even today, buying a luxury item is often reframed by salespeople as creating value. You don't buy a $50,000 watch - you invest in a timepiece that appreciates value like a painting by Van Gogh.

After Lydia worked her reframing trick, Paul found himself put in the position of having to verify that his conversion of this first Christian in Europe was a genuine experience and that it had made Lydia into a more Christ-like devotee immediately.

Saying "yes" became a value-add proposition *for Paul* because it confirmed his own work. He had to confirm his own value. Also, now, all of these people who admire Lydia, as well as the richest people in town who trusted Lydia, would see that Paul's work in Philippi was worth following.

Most great salespeople learn to do this reframing through trial and error. They practice by failing a thousand times until they find the right words to say. But salespeople can learn to meet these objections head on by preparing for them in advance.

THE WIDOW

Some businesspeople wait for a break, praying that money will simply fall into their laps out of nowhere. This is a bad idea. God-ordained wealth transfers are always work-related and earned by our deeds - even if we are unemployed.

There is a story of a widow in 2nd Kings which reveals this lesson well.

"The wife of a man from the company of the prophets cried out to Elisha, "Your servant my husband is dead, and you know that he revered the Lord. But now his creditor is coming to take my two boys as his slaves."
2 Kings 4:1

In those days, if a man were in debt, and had no means of payment, his children were sold into slavery. So here was a poor widow, whose husband had been a servant to a prophet named Elisha during a turbulent time in Israel's ancient history. Prophets were often ascetic - with no worldly goods whatsoever. Elisha was even worse off than most because he was out of favor with the Temple and Court because Elisha disapproved of the King's political marriage.

This means that Elisha's servants were also out of favor. So when the servant died, he was in debt. Consequently, the creditor was coming for his kids to be sold into slavery until they worked off the debt to the creditor's satisfaction.

The widow goes to the prophet Elisha asking for help. Through no fault of her own she was backed in a financial corner with no way out. Notably, the husband's debt was not miraculously canceled despite how pious he was. Instead, the debt was transferred to the widow, and now she had to use her currency to pay off the debt.

But she had no job. She had no assets. Elisha comes to her house without any money of his own, either. This woman was so poor that she had no food in the house. He asks her what she has that might satisfy the creditors who were on their way. The creditors who were coming with armed guards to put her kids in chains.

"Whatever there is in the house must go towards this debt, so 'tell me what hast thou in the house?'" 2 Kings 4:2.

The prophet Elisha is there to provide her with riches…commensurate with the one currency she had cultivated. Her social network.

The only material object she had in the house was a bit of cooking oil at the bottom of a jar.

Elisha tells her to, "Go around and ask all your neighbors for empty jars. Don't ask for just a few. Then go inside and shut the door behind you and your sons. Pour oil into all the jars, and as each is filled, put it to one side." 2 Kings 4:3.

Elisha promised wealth commensurate with her available currency. Evidently the poor woman's credit was good though her debts were heavy; her neighbors knew she would have paid her creditor if she could, so they were willing to grant her request though they probably wondered why she wanted so many empty vessels.

The woman's sons hurried to bring the neighbor's donated jars to her and she kept pouring. Oil miraculously appeared from the one small jar with the dregs of oil she had in the house. When all the donated jars were full, she said to her son, "Bring me another one."

But he replied, "There is not a jar left," by which means 'in the entire neighborhood.' Only then did the oil stop flowing.

Surrounded by full jars of oil, she asked Elisha what to do next and he said, "Go, sell the oil and pay your debts. You and your sons can live on what is left."

"That is thy first duty; 'pay thy debt,'" 2 Kings 4:7.

How can we do that without income or capital? Blessings in business are connected to what you do—your work, whether it be employment or any other work. We must remember that there is more than one kind of currency and they each have value.

The story of the Widow and the Olive Oil is a representation of the business lesson in the Bible about the value of building your professional network.

As we know, there are four currencies in business. They are, again, in this order of importance:

1. Knowledge
2. People
3. Time
4. Money

Actual cash is the least important kind of currency as we learned from Jesus.

Knowledge and wisdom is the most important kind of currency as we learned from Solomon.

The next most important currency is the one that most people overlook: Your network. If you have good people in your life, if you have worked to build bonds of trust with people, those people can help you make miracles happen.

"Encourage on another and build each other up, just as in fact you are doing." 1 Thessalonians 5:11

PART 2

Business Lessons from The Bible

SIMON THE MAGICIAN

According to Acts 8:9-25, Simon of Samaria was a professional sorcerer. He practiced the magical arts for a fee. He likely did this in the open, in a well-established shop because all the people of Samaria knew who he was and were astonished by miracle powers. He was no mythical Merlin, no con-artist, he was a magician. He was making money with his powers.

What does this Bible passage have to teach us about business best practices? We must read the relevant passage through a business lens:

"Now there was a man named Simon, who formerly was practicing magic in the city and astonishing the people of Samaria, claiming to be someone great; and they all, from smallest to greatest, were giving attention to him, saying, "This man is what is called the Great Power of God." And they were giving him attention because he had for a long time astonished them with his magic arts."
Acts 8:9

What happens next in the story is that Philip, a missionary evangelist, travels to Samaria to tell stories about the miracles attributed to Jesus of Nazareth, and how non-sorcerers could also produce miracles if the practitioner was baptized in the name of Jesus the Nazarene:

"But when they believed Philip preaching the good news about the kingdom of God and the name of Jesus Christ, they were being baptized, men and women alike. Even Simon himself believed; and after being baptized, he continued on with Philip, and as he observed signs and great miracles taking place, he was constantly amazed." Acts 13.

It would seem then that Philip got a bit carried away because, next, when word gets back to the home office in Jerusalem that one of the seven evangelist Deacons might be claiming to perform miracles himself, they sent Peter and John to go set the record straight.

Philip's job was merely to baptize these people, not imbue then with the power of the Holy Spirit - only by becoming a full member of the sect (with corresponding tithing) could fill one with the power of God...the one exception to this rule was reserved for Jesus' original twelve apostles, who did have the power to bless audiences with the Holy Spirit and perform miracles.

Peter and John arrive and tell the crowd that they couldn't perform miracles yet because they had simply been baptized. Then they began laying their hands on the people, and said that these individuals were, indeed, receiving the Holy Spirit.

"Now when Simon saw that the Spirit was bestowed through the laying on of the apostles' hands, he offered them money, saying, "Give this authority to me as well, so that everyone on whom I lay my hands may receive the Holy Spirit." Acts 14-19

Essentially, Simon tried to buy his way into the C-Suite of this growing sect, he wanted the power to use the Holy Spirit to perform miracles just like the Apostles were growing famous for doing. It just so happens that at this time, Peter the Apostle was well known along the coastal cities for healing Aeneas and raising Tabitha from the dead.

"But Peter said to him, "May your silver perish with you, because you thought you could obtain the gift of God with money! You have no part or portion in this matter, for your heart is not right before God. Therefore repent of this wickedness of yours, and pray the Lord that, if possible, the intention of your heart may be forgiven you. For I see that you are in the gall of bitterness and in the bondage of iniquity." Acts 20

Peter saw Simon as a competitor who merely wanted to fold Jesus into his own sorcery business. However, the burgeoning Jesus enterprise, as run by Peter, had no intention of diluting its shares by bringing on a new Apostle for a little of Simon's silver.

The lesson here is that Simon the Magician should not have tried to add the powers of Jesus to his own menu of service offerings. A business person must know what kind of business they are engaged in and focus on being the best at offering that service or product -- in other words, do not dilute your brand with too many products of a different nature.

And another lesson here is that Peter was right to not let his sect's product, as it were, get debased by allowing it to be distributed - or in the case of Simon...sold, likely - by a non-franchisee.

After this incident, Peter and John took Philip out of Samaria, where there were too many people like Simon who had heard that anyone could perform magic as long as the incantation was done in Jesus' name. That was decidedly not the goal of Peter's growing sect. Philip was reassigned to Gaza, far in the south.

It was there, on a desert road between Egypt and Jerusalem, that Philip met the Ethiopian Treasurer from the Court of Sheba. This wealthy man, with access to untold fortunes, was traveling away from Jerusalem back home to Africa after having done business with the Temple in Jerusalem.

THE ETHIOPIAN TREASURER

The story of Philip and the Ethiopian Treasurer contains many business lessons about salesmanship and customer acquisition.

In Acts 8:26-40 we meet the Ethiopian Treasurer from Biblical Sheba. In more ancient times the Queen of Sheba traveled to Solomon's Jerusalem to establish trade because the African nation of Ethiopia was a major producer of incense for temple rituals.

This trade was extremely lucrative for Ethiopia and the man in charge of that Treasury just happened to take the road where Philip was working.

Philip waited by the side of the road hoping for passersby to proselytize, Philip sees a royal Ethiopian chariot and immediately runs after it.

"And he arose and went; and behold, there was an Ethiopian eunuch, a court official of Candace, queen of the Ethiopians, who was in charge of all her treasure; and he had come to Jerusalem to worship. And he was returning and sitting in his chariot" Acts 8:27.

Philip's business instinct to pursue this lead is right. A royal Ethiopian chariot could mean that this is likely a wealthy person - a potential prime customer for an evangelist like Philip.

Philip's sales instincts and quick action create an opportunity. It is likely that as the eunuch's dealings with Jerusalem were exclusively with the Temple for his business, meaning that he probably had not heard of the rumors rumbling in the poorer quarters of town about Jesus.

"And when Philip had run up, he heard him reading Isaiah the prophet, and said, "Do you understand what you are reading?" And he said, "Well, how could I, unless someone guides me?" And he invited Philip to come up and sit with him" Acts 8:30.

LISTENING IN A MEETING

It is said in business that success comes when preparation meets luck -- by chance, the Ethiopian court official was sitting in his chariot reading a newly purchased Hebrew text, the book of Isaiah. This was the lucky opportunity that Philip came upon. Thankfully, Philip was prepared for this opportunity thanks to his longtime study of Jewish scripture.

"Now the passage of Scripture which he was reading was this: "He was led as a sheep to slaughter; and as a lamb before its shearer is silent, so he does not open his mouth. In humiliation his judgment was taken away; who shall relate his generation? For his life is removed from the Earth." Acts 8:32

Next, Philip begins his sale by solving a problem. Being helpful for free earns trust and gives a deeper connection for the true sales pitch. This is the spirit behind the business practice of offering free samples, and 'comping' initial sessions, and the like. There is no need for a business to be exclusively predatory, in fact, the best business practices flourish in the context of helping customers in a beneficent manner.

"And the eunuch answered Philip and said, "Please tell me, of whom does the prophet say this? Of himself, or of someone else?" And Philip opened his mouth, and beginning from this Scripture he preached Jesus to him. Acts 8:34

Philip's answer was to proclaim Jesus as the Messiah promised in this mysterious ancient prophecy of Isaiah. Scripturally, this is notable because this is the first time that Isaiah chapter 53 was specifically indicated as a messianic prophecy!

Philip's identification of the One of whom Isaiah wrote as Jesus of Nazareth was an insight that opened the door to much further apostolic preaching among observant Jews. This was a huge breakthrough for Ministers of Jesus' story.

"And as they went along the road they came to some water; and the eunuch said, "Look! Water! What prevents me from being baptized?" And he ordered the chariot to stop; and they both went down into the water, Philip as well as the eunuch; and he baptized him." Acts 8:36

Philip made the sale, so to speak. A rich Gentile who would likely bring back home to Ethiopia this news from Jerusalem that was being suppressed by the Sanhedrin. The growth of the Christian movement in Ethiopia can be traced to this moment. But Philip came away from this meeting with something even greater than a rich foreigner who was on board with the growing Jesus enterprise, Philip had discovered that Isaiah 53 was a great way to reach devout Jews. Philip needed to contact his leadership in Jerusalem.

"And when they came up out of the water, the Spirit of the Lord snatched Philip away; and the eunuch saw him no more, but went on his way rejoicing. But Philip found himself at Azotus; and as he passed through he kept preaching the gospel to all the cities, until he came to Caesarea." Acts 8:39

If we hazard a guess that the Ethiopian court official had indeed heard rumors about the cult of Jesus while he was in Jerusalem, these stories would have been told by Temple Officials like the Sanhedrin, Jerusalem's supreme rabbinic court - the very faction who despised the zealot reformers.

So the Ethiopian would only have heard negative propaganda, likely a story about another one of the seven Deacons named Stephen who had been recently stoned to death for blasphemy. If only Stephen had been armed with this specific scripture!

Philip made the choice to leave his post in the south of the Levant. He journeyed north again, back to where more Jews lived, believing that armed with Isaiah 53 he had a great new insight for the growing sect of Jesus.

The early Church needed it badly because at that time, the Apostles were wary of preaching much more in or near Jerusalem, for fear of more evangelists like Stephen being executed by the Sanhedrin.

WHAT PHILIP LEARNED

In the coming years, according to Acts 21:8–9, Philip remained in the port town of Caesarea where he was later visited by Paul the Apostle and his travel companion; at that time "he had four daughters, virgins, which did prophesy."

This could be interpreted to mean that Philip learned from the whole Simon the Sorcerer ordeal that it was a good business idea to diversify your product offerings so long as the product or service did not dilute your original business plan. If you have the opportunity to do various business dealings, spinning up multiple LLCs to do those various tasks would be preferable to building a single, muddied, busy buffet company which would only dilute and degrade the brand identity of your company.

Essentially, be good at one thing. Get great at it. And if you have an idea for a second thing, make it a second thing - separate. Philip's daughter's soothsaying was not done under the auspices of the church of Peter, nor in the name of Jesus. It was a different business - and that was a good business practice that Philip learned along the line - likely from how Peter treated Simon the Sorcerer.

When Peter visited his Deacons in Caesarea, his visit became known to the occupying soldiers who were often working with Jewish leaders to stamp out any trace of rebellion - this includes Christians. So Peter moved on to a nearby town called Joppa. No sooner had Peter arrived in Joppa at the home of Simon the Tanner, that Peter received a message from Caesarea that a prominent Roman Centurion named Cornelius was asking for him. But that story is a different chapter.

"Whoever heeds instruction is on the path to life, but he who rejects reproof leads others astray."
Proverbs 10:17

THE PRODIGAL SON

The story of a rebellious son who decides to leave his family and waste all his inheritance on worthless trifles is usually thought of as a story of unconditional love and the value of forgiveness.

It was only when the wastrel son didn't have any money left that he realizes his error and comes back to his father:

"Father, I have sinned against heaven and against you. I am no longer worthy to be called your son." Luke 15:21

This story is hard to connect with for most business people because we like to associate themselves with the older son. The diligent hard-working son who stays on the farm and works every day with dad. The one who worked to run the business while his younger brother was off gallivanting around. Naturally, business people would see what happens next with the prodigal son and feel bitter.

The prodigal son comes back, penniless, having thrown away half of the family fortune, and asks to be allowed to live on the farm and work for his room and board like any other worker - no longer as a son. He admits he had given away that honor.

His father welcomes him home with open arms. The father even throws a party for the irresponsible son. This makes the responsible son so mad that he refuses to come to the party. The responsible son feels neglected, he doesn't understand why his father had never thrown him a party in appreciation for having stayed and for having remained responsible for all those years.

The business lessons in this parable are hard to hear for many of us who are the responsible ones. But we can learn a few things about the father's relationship with his sons.

The father is not the kind of boss who ever lavishes praise on good work. In fact when the younger son asks for his inheritance early the father emotionlessly does the transaction.

It is possible that this cold, impersonal, aloofness was also the nature of the father's relationship with the prodigal son before he left. It is possible that pressure to perform destroyed both sons' sense of intimacy with their father.

One lesson that the older responsible son probably learned in this moment, and a lesson we can take from his experience, is that the squeaky wheel gets the grease.

You need to advocate for yourself sometimes when you do not enjoy a close and trusting relationship with the boss. Nobody is going to argue for you to get the raise you deserve if you're not a member of a union. Within reason you have to complain about your compensation, and you have to fight for recognition that reflects your contributions.

We don't like thinking about this part of the story of the prodigal son for a similar reason to why we find it so hard to demand the raise we deserve. It feels ugly. It feels transactional. But sometimes that is our relationship with the boss, or our father. In times like these it is necessary to be the squeaky wheel.

There are also lessons we can learn from the actions of the prodigal son. While he's away, as soon as he runs out of money he learns that money is not always the answer. Which is exactly too late. This son had demanded his inheritance early, when he was too young to have learned the value of hard work or the secrets of what to do with wealth.

His inheritance was supposed to have been earned after working for his father for years. It was supposed to come after years of knowledge. He skipped right to the reward -- no wonder he did not have a strong enough foundation upon which to build a life. Without having worked for his money, the gold was without value to his life. The wastrel son splurged all of his money away.

His inheritance was not satisfying or long-lasting because it was not earned. The prodigal son learns that money earned through hard work is greatly prized and truly valuable. However, wealth unearned lacks the value of effort - the effort which should have gone into making the money in the first place.

Because he had not lived the time and effort to earn his money, he did not recognize its value and so he frivolously wasted it away on parties. Parties, it should be noted, which had nothing to celebrate, so even they too must have come to feel hollow.

When the prodigal son returns, he tells his father that he learned the value of things. He recognizes that in his youthful ignorance he did not value his position of "son" to his father - nor of his position of worker to his boss. He acknowledges that he now seeks to work and will do as any other worker does, working daily for his room and board.

This doesn't strike the father as a ploy to get back into good graces with the boss. The father sees that his prodigal son is being genuine. The boy has actually learned, finally, the lesson of wealth which should take a lifetime to learn.

The party that the father throws to celebrate is not just because the spoiled son has returned, but because the son has learned a huge life lesson which has made him ready to reinvest in the family firm.

And what about the responsible son? Is he wrong to feel slighted? Of course. He probably feels insulted.

But consider the father - as a metaphor for God, the most important character in the parable of the Prodigal Son is the father. We want our authority figures to love us but sometimes they are cold and impersonal. What they should be sometimes is filled with compassion and enthusiasm. We see this not just in the way the father celebrates his lost son's personal growth, but also in the way the father is said to be overtaken with compassion for his prodigal son.

Usually the elder of a family sits under a shade and the family members come to them in reverence. But the Bible tells us that the father goes running to the prodigal son and embraces him. In a world of elder worship, for the elder of the house to grovel like that was the most shameful thing the father of the family could do. But propriety did not matter at that moment. It could be seen that the father also finally learned a lesson about showing his true emotions.

The elder of the family is willing to make himself look like a fool toward the very one who committed the greatest offense. At an allegorical level, this is telling us how much God loves us, yes, but it is also a lesson about being a good manager. Perhaps the father realized that his previous frigid attitude towards his sons was a terrible mistake.

Based on how the older son talks to his father later, we can assume that his father's aloofness colored his relationship with the older son too because we are told that the father "pleads" with his older son. He would not need to plead if his working relationship with his older son was more open and featured a full exchange of ideas.

Instead the father pleads with the good son:

"'My son,' the father said, 'you are always with me, and everything I have is yours. But we had to celebrate and be glad, because this brother of yours was dead and is alive again; he was lost and is found.'" Luke 15:31-32

We are not told whether the older son ever joined the party. He should have joined the party because the party was for the future of the family firm. How should workers feel about their peers who slack off or get treatment that feels unfair? The father assures the older son that now he has his brother back and he has a business partner back. It is a cause for celebration.

If the prodigal son had returned but had not learned anything of value, it is highly doubtful that the father would throw a party. Perhaps the older son should believe the father and see that everything is different now. The workforce will be forever changed for the better. And while they will never get back the lost time that the younger son squandered, they have everyday going forward to enjoy the success that this newly reunited team will surely enjoy.

When we start off in business we think we need to be doing good work to please the boss. The same is true about how many people think of their relationship with God...they believe that when they have money they'll pay back those blessings by building hospitals and alleviating the pain and problems of humankind...for God.

It turns out we should be doing things "because of" God. We should do good work that makes profit because of the policies put in place by our boss. The boss should have created a system whereby the actions which the business takes are exactly the kinds of things that will alleviate the pain and problems of humankind. In this way, we are doing good things because of God, because of the boss.

When we are lucky enough to work for an employer like this, or when we learn how to become a boss like this - building a business as beneficial as this - it is like being in a wonderful relationship with God. We realize that we are doing great things with God, with our boss because, in truth, we are partners.

These are the subterranean lessons of the story of the Prodigal Son.

PARABLE OF THE TALENTS

In Matthew 25:14, Jesus tells the story of a rich businessman who prepares to go on a journey by calling his three servants together and entrusting them with his property.

To one of his workers he gave five talents worth of money, to another two talents of money, and to the last one he gave one talent... "to each according to his ability."

This means he gave the most money to his most capable worker. Before leaving, the businessman told all three workers to use the money wisely in service of the enterprise.

The worker who had received the five talents went at once and traded with them, buying and selling items with neighboring merchants and he was able to make five talents in profit. The worker who was moderately capable used his two talents and earned two talents more with trades and sales.

But the one who received only one talent thought only about losing the one precious talent of coins he had been given so he went and buried his master's money in the ground to keep it safe.

When the master returns he says "well done" to the first two, calling them "good and faithful servants." But to the last one who buried the money so as to not lose it, the master rages. The fearful worker claims that he thought about how his boss can be "a hard man" and that's why he tried only to protect the money.

The master calls this worker "wicked and slothful."

"Then you ought to have invested my money with the bankers, and at my coming I should have received what was my own with interest."
Matthew 25:27

He says even if you had just put the money in the bank it would have earned at least some interest, but instead you did nothing. So the boss takes the money back and gives it to his top earning employee for him to work with next time.

This shows us that promotions and pay raises are based squarely on achievement. A business is run as a meritocracy. The man with five talents earns five more and is given more responsibility and authority as a result of his success.

Jesus describes the businessman distributing wealth "to each according to his ability" -- not "to each according to his need." This businessman believed that his employees were more than servants, they were like partners, all of them trying to maximize the business results.

The lesson here is that if you operate out of fear, you will be cast out - fired. As a business owner, we must cast out our own fear, and as an employee we must ask if we are doing all that we can to maximize the business' output?

Seen one way, God gives us all one opportunity: Life. What will you do with it? What should we do if we are not given much? What should we do if we are given the least? Many of us do not inherit any property or trust funds. The answer boils down to "act!" We must not be paralyzed by fear.

We must act in a prudent and considered way, but we cannot waste time. Jesus literally states that the easiest path to success is to have your money work for you by earning interest. Nowadays a safe mutual fund is the easiest path to success.

We also learn that the first two workers, those who were given the most money to invest or work with went to work immediately.

Businesspeople with talent do not dither with fear and indecision, they act.

So let's sum up. In this story, achievement rather than mere effort is rewarded. No one cares if you "worked hard" or if you "tried hard" - the businessman cares about results. He makes business decisions based on data. Laziness and fear is punished rather than tolerated.

The best result from these three workers would be to have taken a moderate portion of the money and -- based on the admonition from the angry businessman to his last worker -- invested in safe bonds or conservative index fund. The next largest chunk of money is used to optimize the current sales funnel while the largest amount is reinvested in the business and with their partners.

CAMEL THROUGH THE EYE OF THE NEEDLE

An oft-quoted passage that might not sit well with those looking to amass and preserve wealth is one of Jesus' tricky translation traps:

"It is easier for a camel to go through the eye of a needle than for a rich man to enter the kingdom of God." Mark 10:25

First, context: Jesus didn't say this out of the blue. He said it when a young rich man approached him and asked him how he can "inherit eternal life." This was a question about inheritance and estate planning.

So what is Jesus really saying here? That depends on which translation of the Bible we are reading.

For 1,100 years it's been suggested that the word "camel" in this passage was a mistranslation where the Aramaic kámēlos, or "camel" was written instead of kámilos, meaning "knot." Translations from ancient Syriac-language versions of the Bible run into this same translation problem.

Can you get a knot through the eye of a needle? Yes, if you unknot the line first - if you undo the binding, yes, there is nothing keeping the line from passing through the eye of a needle. That's if the needle is metaphorical. But what if Jesus is being serious?

Also yes, "Eye of the Needle" was the name of a particularly narrow gate through the Walls of Jerusalem

In Jerusalem, the gates into the city are wide enough to drive a car through. But when the gate is closed, it is literally a wooden wall - but in that wall there is a smaller door with a sliding window for eyes to peek out of. This smaller door is the size of one person. The little door in the gate wall is called "the Eye of the Needle."

This door-within-a-wall was designed for security reasons so that a man would have to unload his camel of all that it was carrying and then carefully lead his camel through this small gate. It was a slow and quite difficult task. You can see how it would be difficult for a camel to get through that door, but not impossible.

The most important thing to take from this is that the camel would need to be unloaded. Camels are pack animals, goods and valuables are hung from their sides, making a fully-loaded camel extremely wide.

The camel could certainly get into heaven, so to speak, but it would need to leave its wealth outside. Traders had to unload their goods, pay tax and then they were given access to the markets. For a trader, this must have been like entering heaven.

So either way we look at this translation debate, whether about unloading the camel or untying the knot, the real point of the story remains the same; We cannot take our wealth with us to heaven when we die. We have to write a will that includes a plan for how your wealth will continue to work when you're gone.

What will it be working towards? All of the same things it works for now. It will employ your workforce, it will reward your investors, it will support your family. Indeed, these should be the goals of wise business investment while a business person is still alive. We all want to be able to financially support our lifestyles with passive income while we're alive to enjoy time and space for contentment.

Jesus is saying what we do in life should be the same as what is done when we're gone. It is a story about estate planning. From the beginning, the question was about "inheritance" and Jesus' answer was about inheritance. Write a will today.

"An inheritance gained hurriedly at the beginning will not be blessed in the end." Proverbs 20:21

78

MONEY IS <u>NOT</u> THE ROOT OF ALL EVIL

One of the common refrains against capitalist society is the oft-quoted line from the Bible: "money is the root of all evil." But this quip is nearly always accompanied by a grave misunderstanding of the entire passage. Let us dispel this common mistake with a quick lesson.

The offending verse is surely provocative:

"But those who desire to be rich fall into temptation, into a snare, into many senseless and harmful desires that plunge people into ruin and destruction. For the love of money is a root of all kinds of evils. 1 Timothy 6:9

So technically, no, Paul doesn't say money is the root of all evil. He says "loving" money is the root of all kinds of evil. The love of money can motivate any evil on this Earth - there is no sin that cannot be committed for the sake of money.

One again, there is no sin that cannot be committed for the sake of money. That is what is meant by "root."

But firstly, we need to know the context. The author, the Apostle Paul, is writing to one of his pastors Timothy, shortly after his own release from Roman prison in Macedonia. Paul was writing to Timothy in Ephesus, a wealthy city in what is now western Turkey. Paul discovered that in his absence, many Deacons and missionaries in Ephesus were perverting the message of Jesus and so Timothy's branch of the early Church needed a reprimand.

Paul's middle-managers such as preachers, deacons, missionaries - depending on the stage of the Church's growth - were incredibly important as Christianity spread towards Europe. These individuals were like salesmen, but they were also like Branch Managers, and Brand Ambassadors. What Paul is saying to Timothy is that the manner with which preachers present themselves to the public must be above reproach.

The book of Timothy is Paul's pep-talk to Timothy and advice about how to spot a bad preacher and why it's important to stop them. To paraphrase a 19th Century American Business proverb: there may very well be "a sucker born every minute," but a salesperson should not go around calling everyone they meet a sucker.

"Now the end of the commandment is charity." 1 Timothy 1:5

Your business must perform a needed service, offered in the spirit of helpfulness. Additionally, we business people need to love what we do with a pure heart and sincerity because if you are an exploitative Brand Ambassador, or a middle-manager who has clearly given up on giving back, one who has abandoned the attitude of helpfulness, if you are obviously in it only for love of money...your customers will see this truth about you, and your congregation (branch or franchise location, as it were) will wither and die.

Without sincerity, it is easy to become shallow micromanagers who are only concerned with outward appearance for the hollow ring of the next sale.

Paul is telling Timothy that too many middle managers appeared as though they were in it simply for power.

If what drives you is solely an obsession with becoming rich, then you are doing it wrong. This is the folly of a greedy heart. The desire for riches is more dangerous than the riches themselves.

There were many godly men in the Bible who were almost unbelievably rich, such as Abraham, David, and Solomon - poor does not mean godly nor rich ungodly.

"And some by longing for money have wandered away from the faith and pierced themselves with many griefs. 1 Timothy 6:10

Paul says many griefs are the fate of those who are driven solely by the love of money: They are never satisfied. And these business people without a strong core, in order to grasp for more riches, will try any foolish idea.

They will waste time and effort grasping at get-rich-quick schemes, they will muddy their operation with the remnants of previous failed attempts, each diluting and diminishing the purity of the enterprise. This flailing about for the next hit is the "useless, foolish" or "senseless and harmful" griefs that Paul refers to. These wastes of effort plunge people into ruin.

It is the people without a strong core who do this. The business people without discipline, the people without a strong belief in the business plan. We need to trust the plan so much that the public sees only that we are full of trust - we are there to help.

"But you, O man of God, flee these things and pursue righteousness, godliness, faith, love, patience, gentleness. 1 Timothy 6:11

Paul is not promoting poverty but encouraging us to focus on what truly matters. What matters is the core of our business plan put into action with a giving heart.

82

THE PASSOVER FEAST

One of the most dramatic moments in the life of Jesus comes just before the Passover holiday. Jesus and his followers are all together to celebrate the Jewish festival with a feast. Suddenly Jesus has this realization, a feeling:

"Jesus knew that the Father had put all things under his power, and that he had come from God and was returning to God; so he got up from the meal, took off his outer clothing, and wrapped a towel around his waist. After that, he poured water into a basin and began to wash his disciples' feet, drying them with the towel that was wrapped around him." John 13:5-5

Jesus realizes that everything is under his authority. He realizes he is the most powerful living thing in the universe. In this exact moment, Jesus knew that God had given him unstoppable powers.

The first thing he does is take off his robe and wash the feet of his apostles and their guests.

This is an amazing lesson to take from the life of Jesus.

When we are the boss, we need to wash people's feet. We need to take on interns and pay them. We need to teach people what we know. We need to take on shadows and let them learn our ways. We need to share our leads. We need to be givers, not takers.

At another time, God says it's time for you to stop believing me, it's time for you to start following me. This represents a mindset shift that we are called to act upon. And it is a mindset shift when we strive to be a better employee too. Our actions will be what matter, not just our intentions.

That may feel risky, but it's not: If your dreams aren't big, it's only because you're not aware of how much God loves you.

And remember always that we can make amends when we fail - and everyone fails at some point. Think of the story of the only two people who betrayed Jesus: Judas Iscariot who sold him out and Peter who denied him three times.

Judas took the silver, cashed out too soon and hung himself afterwards. Judas' betrayal was short-sighted and his reaction was that of a coward.

Peter's failure was just as deliberate, he had two chances to make up for his denial of Jesus. He failed. But his reaction to this failure was to dedicate the rest of his life to spreading Jesus' message.

Peter was deemed the rock upon which Jesus would build his Church. Judas failed and didn't grow. Peter failed but he chose to grow from it.

When we lead we should lead like Jesus. When we become powerful we should act like Jesus in his humility. When we fail we should fail like Peter. We should act like Peter in his great adjustment and his persistence. And we must always, always serve.

85

PART 3

The Word of God for Wealth Creation

"The heart of man plans his way, but the Lord establishes his steps." Proverbs 16:9

BUILD A BUSINESS PLAN AND STICK TO IT

The book of Proverbs is full of wisdom about how a thoughtful business person should approach the day. Businesspeople are literally told by God to ponder their path before setting out. In other words, "Plan ahead."

"Ponder the path of your feet; then all your ways will be sure"
Proverbs 4:26.

Planning ahead for your finances and planning wisely in your business acts is a common refrain in the Bible.

Your business plan must be a reflection of your values and it must factor in your short-term and long-term costs.

"Suppose one of you wants to build a tower. Will he not first sit down and estimate the cost to see if he has enough money to complete it?" Luke 14:28

In the early stages of business planning, track your cash flow and burn rate and always factor in unforeseen costs.

The task of imagining unforeseen costs takes some imagination but it also can be accomplished by following closely what setbacks befall similar businesses. Read and study the business trades. Ask successful people questions about their businesses and the difficulties that they've overcome.

"The wise save to take care of needs down the road."
Proverbs 21:20.

Diligent, thoughtful planning leads to "abundance" Proverbs 21:5. Additionally, planning involves being realistic about your financial situation, because unrealistic wheel-spinning and "Idle talk" (Proverbs 14:23) or "wishful thinking" (Proverbs 28:19) will lead only to poverty and want.

Likewise, failing to stick with your plan is a sure way to fail. When given an opportunity we must act. Procrastination will doom us: "Sluggards do not plow in season; so at harvest time they look but find nothing." Proverbs 20:4

As Proverbs goes on to explain: "The wise plan ahead to avoid dangers into which the simple keep going" Proverbs 22:3.

But why do we plan? For the future: Because "riches do not last forever," so careful pondering and planning are required to provide "for yourself and your family" Proverbs 27:23-27.

REDUCE DEBT

The Bible warns us about debt from thousands of years ago, and one of the best things most of us can do is to follow its old, wise advice.

"Debt only empowers the wicked and drags down hope for your prosperity," as the Bible says. It can be true that most banks only leech off small business owners.

Those ancient warnings against money lenders are just as relevant today for households that have maxed out credit cards, sought the immediate gratification of rent-to-own plans, or taken on mortgages beyond their means.

"The rich rules over the poor, and the borrower becomes the lender's slave." Proverbs 22:7

Those who leapt into subprime mortgages they couldn't afford or have a car in danger of being repossessed might have been spared a lot of grief if they contemplated the guidance in Proverbs 22:26 to "not be a man who strikes hands in pledge or puts up security for debts; if you lack the means to pay, your very bed will be snatched from under you."

As for those who profit from debt, banks may not be inclined to heed this warning found in Exodus: "If you lend money to my people, to the poor among you, you are not to act as a creditor to him; you shall not charge him interest."

"The wicked borrow and never repay, but the godly are generous givers" Psalm 37:21.

There are times when you lend someone money that they would start avoiding you instead of paying you back, and you'll almost never see them again. Don't be like those people.

If you're still in debt, pay what you owe. You may not know if your debtor is also having money problems.

Paying your debt shows that you value your relationship, thus showing your character. Just as we should be smart on purpose in public, we should be faithful, always.

SAVE MORE, BUT DON'T HOARD

The rate at which people save money today is so low that it could nearly qualify as a rounding error.

Scared into reducing debt by recession and interest rate hikes, consumers are a bit more serious about tucking aside some of each paycheck. Students of the Bible would certainly see this as a lesson that has long been stressed in Scripture.

Corinthians 16:2 offers this advice for sticking to a savings plan: "On the first day of every week each one of you is to put aside and save, as he may prosper, so that no collections be made when I come."

"Four things on Earth are small, yet they are extremely wise: Ants are creatures of little strength, yet they store up their food in the summer" Proverbs 30:24-25.

An emergency fund is a Biblical principle. Just like how ants store food during summer in preparation for the winter, we should also prepare during our good season to have something reserved when the time of financial trials comes.

However, we should not hoard our gains. We need to reinvest in ourselves. We need to invest in a diverse portfolio, we need to pay our workers commensurate with how well their work for us has led to our growth.

It's been said that "money is like manure, it's only good if you spread it around." Not only is hoarded money the "wicked and slothful" sin of the least gifted servant in Jesus' Parable of the Talents, hoarded money is the sign of a stagnant and closed mind. Businesspeople like this do not succeed beyond the next market downturn.

Another part of the Bible is about one thing we should do once each growing season. In other words, once a year, before the busy season is wrapped we should:

"Bring the whole tithe into the storehouse, that there may be food in my house. Test me in this," says the Lord Almighty, "and see if I will not throw open the floodgates of heaven and pour out so much blessing that there will not be room enough to store it."
Malachi 3:10

The lesson is to reinvest in yourself one out of twelve times that you would normally put aside some income as savings. When you put the whole tithe of that month in the storehouse, we are told you will get greater returns.

WATCH YOUR CREDIT RATING

As for those considering just walking away from an underwater mortgage, the Bible hands out some stern guidance:

"The wicked borrows and does not pay back, but the righteous is gracious and gives." Psalm 37:2

Not only is it a bad idea, it is wicked! We are also warned:

"It is better that you should not vow than that you should vow and not pay." Ecclesiastes 5:5

If you find that you want to take out a loan, be mindful that you are not simply papering over poor fundamentals. The matter is one of proper planning ahead of time and prudent planning as the business is ongoing.

"A tithe of everything from the land, whether grain from the soil or fruit from the trees, belongs to the Lord; it is holy to the Lord." Leviticus 27:30-31

The act of saving has to add value. Is it serving the underlying business? Is it adding value? It needs to vest because if we try to exercise prematurely we have wasted the value:

"Whoever would redeem any of their tithe must add a fifth of the value to it." Leviticus 27:30-31

This is a recipe for a good credit rating. Do not cash out too soon. And when you do pay off a credit card, do so with cash reserves on hand - prove that they are liquid by extending your credit limit, even if you no longer use the card. That is preferable to closing a credit card.

The fundamentals of good credit have not changed in 3000 years. It's not too late to learn them.

PAY YOUR TAXES

Taxes are like membership dues in a club. To be a member of the club of your country there is a yearly bill. If you don't like the perks of your club, you can move to a different place with better perks.

In truth, the regulatory burden for businesses in the United States is lower than many other countries in the world. These are just facts - facts as plain as a tax bill. Pay your tax bill.

"Render to Caesar the things that are Caesar's; and to God the things that are God's" Matthew 22:21

God does not want you to cheat on your tax bill or hide assets to pay less. He commands us to pay all our bills.

It is correct that you will have many bills throughout a business year. If your country's government does not offer citizens government-provided healthcare, then your tax bill may be lower -- but your healthcare company bills and your health insurance bills, and your prescription drug bills, and your ambulance bills will likely end up cumulatively higher. High enough that in the final analysis, the lower costs to live and work elsewhere makes moving worthwhile. Remember that Abraham moved in order to thrive.

On the other hand, the Bible also tells us to fight for our Nation's defense. This doesn't necessarily mean serving in the military. The Book of Job tells us that fighting for your Nation to enact more righteous and caring laws and a more just system of alleviating poverty is also what God wants of us.

It can be argued that if the quality-of-life of citizens in your country continues to drop below that of other countries, as we are seeing in the United States, God would like you to not leave…but instead to stay and fight for the laws to be more like Job of Utz - caring for the labor conditions of all workers and protecting them against exploitation by wicked businessmen.

Either way, you have to pay all your bills. Including your tax bill:

"Give everyone what you owe him. If you owe taxes, pay taxes; if revenue, then revenue; if respect, then respect; if honor, then honor." Romans 13:7

We must stay on top of our debt, taxes, credit cards, loans -- fit the recurring payments into our monthly budget. Staying on top of our costs takes work. Staying true to our word is a daily chore that becomes second nature.

BE A GOOD BOSS FOR AN ETHICAL COMPANY

The values of your business are an extension of your family's values. As an employer, are you looking for ways to exploit people? Either by trimming your payroll, reducing benefits, or overworking your staff in the name of increased productivity?

Are you undermining your company's strength and soiling your own soul by outsourcing manufacturing to sweatshops in a foreign land? Are your vendors so overworked that some workers are killing themselves?

Some people who think they are blameless are the ones to blame. The Bible warns us that we should start trying to earn the respect of our workers and the respect of our competitors' workers too.

"Look! The wages you failed to pay the workmen who mowed your fields are crying out against you. The cries of the harvesters have reached the ears of the Lord Almighty." James 5:4.

We are similarly warned by even more ancient prophecies:

"He who oppresses the poor to make more for himself or who gives to the rich, will only come to poverty." Proverbs 22:16

As for employees, working hard is a recipe for success. Proverbs 10:4 puts it this way: "A slack hand causes poverty, but the hand of the diligent makes rich." This lesson also comes back to us in the form of the Parable of the Talents.

As with the Book of Job, being a good boss means caring for the wellbeing of your workers and even of other workers who are mistreated. We are told:

"For Scripture says, "Do not muzzle an ox while it is treading out the grain," and "The worker deserves his wages." 1 Timothy 5:18

Do not muzzle your workers. Do not stifle their creativity, do not mistreat them or disapprove of their contributions. They want to be respected and all workers appreciate good wages. Think of your workers as an asset not a liability. Treat them well and they will appreciate in value as assets.

When you unleash their creativity, they may surprise you and help you completely reinvent your business for the better as Joseph did for the Pharaoh. Let them partner in your firm's success.

BUILD YOUR PROFESSIONAL NETWORK

The story of the Widow and the Olive Oil is an ancient parable that reveals the value of building your professional network. In the world of business we come to understand that really there are four kinds of currency, this lesson is so important that it bears repeating The four currencies are, in this order of importance:

1. Knowledge
2. People
3. Time
4. Money

Actual cash is the least important kind of currency. Knowledge and wisdom is the most important kind of currency. People are the next most important currency and this is the one that is most often overlooked.

"People" or, a robust professional network, can solve problems of scale - if the job is too big for just you and your wisdom alone do the work with other people.

"People" solves problems of scope - if the job is beyond your area of expertise alone. You can always partner with other people, or contract with them, or study from the people who have knowledge which you may not have.

"People" solves the problem of time even, if you are falling short on a tight deadline, you can throw more people at the project.

"People" can even solve the problem of cash flow - but only if you have met and cultivated investors or a banker who believes in your business plan.

All of this is to say that the secret to much business success is to prioritize people. The art of building bridges with people, the art of collaboration with people, strengthening your network is a very valuable lesson we find in the Bible. The Bible knows this secret and teaches it to us:

"I tell you, use worldly wealth to gain friends for yourselves, so that when it is gone, you will be welcomed into eternal dwellings."
Luke 16:9

We should not only use our worldly wealth, but every kind of currency to build the very professional networks that are so often the difference-maker between success and failure.

AVOID PONZI SCHEMES

Even the ancient writers who crafted The Bible's many books knew something that many investors targeted by fraudsters seem to forget -- if something looks too good to be true, it probably is.

Proverbs 14:15 cautions that, "The naive believes everything, but the sensible man considers his steps."

Think you can get rich quick? Think again:

"Dishonest money dwindles away, but he who gathers money little by little makes it grow." Proverbs 13:11.

Get rich quick schemes sound great on the surface but when you dig deeper, they are usually promoted by people who are being dishonest, whether they realize it or not.

Just because someone promises massive returns backed up with testimonials from others doesn't mean you might have the same experience.

The con men themselves don't get off easy. Proverbs 13:11 admonishes that, "Wealth obtained by fraud dwindles, but the one who gathers by labor increases it."

More direct is the lack of wiggle room found in the commandment, "Thou shalt not steal." Getting involved in a get-rich-quick scheme or gambling for income is not advisable for your wallet or your soul.

"Work willingly at whatever you do, as though you were working for the Lord rather than for people. Remember that the Lord will give you an inheritance as your reward, and that the Master you are serving is Christ. But if you do what is wrong, you will be paid back for the wrong you have done. For God has no favorites."
Colossians 3:23-25

DIVERSIFY YOUR PORTFOLIO AND ASSETS

The Bible doesn't delve too deeply into portfolio rebalancing or the value of emerging markets. But in a far more poetic way, it does suggest a careful distribution of your assets.

"Divide your investments to seven, or even to eight, for you do not know what misfortune may occur on the Earth," Ecclesiastes 11:2

This book of the Bible is sharing an investment lesson from King Solomon himself, the wealthiest man of his era.

Investing your money in several different types of assets will help you protect your money. It smooths out your returns and minimizes risk versus burying all your investments in one asset.

The common advice to never put all your eggs in one basket is reflected in the Bible. It is crucial that you put your investments in multiple asset classes. By diversifying, you spread your risk if something were to happen to one of your investments.

For example, if you invested all your assets in a meme stock, and you missed the short sale trading hour before either the market crashed or the stock dropped back down to a low fundamental price, you will have a hard time recovering your losses no matter how long you hold the stock.

An example of diversification is investing in unrelated assets like real estate, the stock market, mutual funds, and other financial vehicles.

The truth is that when the value of one type of asset tanks for a while, very commonly other assets may do better because of how interconnected the lending markets are and how the insurance industry's rates affect so many other sectors in adversarial ways. When one kind of asset class loses 20%, that value will be somewhere else in the market, spread around in various gains which must equal the 20%.

BELIEVE THE EXPERTS

We all need business mentors. We need to take the counsel of our legal advisors or the advice of our business school professors. Having faith in your business plan is important, but so too is building a business plan that is based on sound fundamentals.

"Without counsel plans fail, but with many advisers they succeed"
Proverbs 15:22.

No one business person can know everything. But also, neither does anyone else know everything. We are all limited, our vision distorted through the lens of our individual experience, and sometimes we might not even know what we don't know.

"The way of a fool is right in his own eyes." Proverbs 12:15.

We all have blind spots and may not realize it:

"Those who trust only in themselves are fools" Proverbs 28:26.

What this is saying to us is that a wise person seeks the advice of many and from varied perspectives. This means talking to experts in fields ranging from investment to customer retention strategies, from the macro to the micro.

"Blessed is the one who finds wisdom, and the one who gets understanding, for the gain from her is better than gain from silver and her profit better than gold. She is more precious than jewels, and nothing you desire can compare with her." Proverbs 3:13-15.

Proverbs pleads for us to remember that wisdom and good counsel is more valuable than simple capital. Additionally, we should search widely for wisdom with an eye seeking "as for hidden treasures" Proverbs 2:4.

Unique insights in business wisdom are worth more than silver, choice gold, and rubies because such intel can lead us to untapped value.

"Whoever ignores instruction despises himself, but he who listens to reproof gains intelligence." Proverbs 15:32

Above all, it is crucial to understand our own shortcomings in business and be willing to not only ask for help but accept the answers offered by our mentors and live by them. Humility in business is a great virtue because it is the main trait that allows us to carry on when the market turns bearish as it always will.

"Poverty and disgrace come to him who ignores instruction, but whoever heeds reproof is honored." Proverbs 3:18

Learn from your mistakes! You can't be a successful investor or business person by going it alone. We all need the help and advice of others if we want to succeed. Whether you seek out a qualified, licensed investment advisor, or you read a lot of books on investing, seeking wise counsel always pays dividends.

How should we know who to trust? Take a page from Jesus' Parable of the Talents. Those who have achieved success and have shown themselves to be highly skilled deserve the most of our faith when it comes to matters of financial advice.

But this point comes with a large caveat: We can only trust them in the way that the Master trusted his Servant in Jesus' parable -- we need to know that the advice-giver is actively working for our success. They could just as easily be leading us astray for their own profits.

Be wary of second-hand advice or free advice from a businessman who we don't know, people whose reputation are that they are willing to exploit others for their own gain. The reality is we may need to pay for expert advice. This means paying for business school or paying for a financial advisor's help. But again, trust the best, and hear the rest.

WRITE A WILL

The first instance of a biblical estate plan goes all the way back to Abraham in the book of Genesis. At God's urging, he left "everything he owned to Isaac" and subsequent heirs all provided a will to dictate how their post-death belongings would be distributed.

The Bible promotes the value of such a legacy:

"A good man leaves an inheritance for his children's children."
Proverbs 13:22

The Apostles of Jesus also talk about the value of building a legacy and planning for our businesses to outlive us for greater success.

"I have seen a grievous evil under the sun: wealth hoarded to the harm of its owners, or wealth lost through some misfortune, so that when they have children there is nothing left for them to inherit."
Ecclesiastes 5:13-14

The act of writing a will attached to your business is a profound moment because if the business lives on after you, it can be an extension of your values and an extension of the labor of your life. Humans are mortal, but corporations can be immortal. And if you have built your business well, meaning it provides a beneficent act without exploiting workers, customers, or natural resources, then the good work of your lifetime can extend through the ages.

WORK HARD AND TRUE

It almost goes without saying that being a successful business person takes hard work. Almost. You have to work diligently at your craft.

"Lazy people are soon poor; hard workers get rich." Proverbs 10:4

But in this day and age, when we constantly hear nonsense about overnight millionaires, remembering the value of diligent action is important.

"Whoever watches the wind will not plant; whoever looks at the clouds will not reap" Ecclesiastes 11:4.

We must *will* ourselves to keep working, no matter what. If you look for economic evidence that suggests a posture of inaction, you will always be able to find it because what you will actually be locating, in many cases, are other timid people.

We need to stay focused on our goal - which is not money for the sake of riches. The goal is to be of great service to your fellow man. Every business provides a service. We have to want to be that, to do that - earnestly.

So much of the Bible is warning us to not try to fake magnanimity. We must find something we love doing genuinely and then find a way to turn it into a business. If what we love doing genuinely is helping people, then we are at an advantage because in that spirit we could do just about anything as a business. But if we have a certain set of skills and only that particular pastime gives us joy, then it is incumbent on us to forge the business plan.

Once we have a business plan, other areas of the Bible warn us to not stray from our core, our goal, our vision for our business. We need discipline to remain committed to our business. The line that best sums up this invaluable lesson is:

"For where your treasure is, there your heart will be also.
Matthew 6:21

To put that wisdom another way, "where your heart is, there your treasure will be."

Do you have an idea for a business that will help new parents? Then stick to it. That business should focus like a laser with all of the love you have for your customer and your idea. Your business should not be diluted by an array of cul-de-sacs, pandering to flash-in-the-pan notions beyond your target audience and your core offering.

"Now this I say, he who sows sparingly will also reap sparingly, and he who sows bountifully will also reap bountifully. 2 Corinthians 9:6

Or, in other words: our wealth is commensurate with how hard we work. This is directly followed by:

"Each one must do just as he has purposed in his heart, not grudgingly or under compulsion, for God loves a cheerful giver.
2 Corinthians 9:7

BE CONTENT

A desperate, grasping business person is likely to fail. Lust for wealth in any form is a kind of blindness. It blocks our vision - our business vision for the "To Market Strategy" we have devised. Very often, what is needed in a volatile marketplace is a cool head and the confidence in our planning. The attitude that will sustain such behavior is "contentment."

"Not that I speak from want, for I have learned to be content in whatever circumstances I am. I know how to get along with humble means, and I also know how to live in prosperity; in any and every circumstance I have learned the secret of being filled and going hungry, both of having abundance and suffering need. I can do all things through Him who strengthens me." Philippians 4:11-13

To 'suffer need' is not just a matter of poverty. Yes, poor people need food and shelter, but when we talk about a "love of money" we're talking about a chronic debilitating "need" that cannot be quenched.

When an obsession with exponential growth takes root, a business person will never be able to maintain their trajectory for long. We live on a finite Earth. This chronic illness of need has a cure: contentment.

Our consumer culture has conditioned us to think that we always have to earn more money to buy more things. We don't need all these things, but we are told that they will make us feel good. This is wrong.

If our business operates only from quarter to quarter we are unable to plan long term. Just as strip-mining our own holdings for a short-term gain is foolish, scrounging for more money by any means necessary is a short-sighted goal that should be avoided.

We need to understand that money is a means to an end, not the end itself. It is essential to know when you have enough. Think of the gambler who is wise enough and prudent enough at the gaming table to remember to only gamble with her winnings - as soon as she earns back her initial buy-in, she literally puts that amount of winnings in her sock, "socks it away" never to be touched again for the rest of the night. She only works with the overage. This wise practice takes discipline.

"No discipline seems pleasant at the time, but painful. Later on, however, it produces a harvest..." Hebrews 12:11

This insight is much like Paul's advice to Timothy the Ephesian:

"Godliness with contentment is great gain. For we brought nothing into the world, and we can take nothing out of it. But if we have food and clothing, we will be content with that. 1 Timothy 6:6-7

Contentment and humility is the beginning of wisdom. The Bible sometimes refers to this as "fear of the Lord."

To be a successful business person takes the bravery to act in the face of great obstacles like Abraham. It takes the focus and refinement of our skills like David. And then like Solomon, once we have humility and contentment, we have wisdom.

With wisdom we can begin to do anything - every kind of success, rich in the blessings of every kind of currency. God knows it. Now so do you.

A Parting Prayer

It is my prayer that anyone who either seeks to start a business or works every day to grow their business will come to know that, just like everything else in life, even our business comes from God.

If we believe that God is our heavenly father, we must also believe that He wants us to grow and learn and succeed. To do these things in our business life, I pray to God that we can all follow The Bible's ways in our work. Only in this way can we honor the gift we were given when we were brought into the world and offered a chance at success.

It is my prayer that we will all capitalize on this piece of good luck which we are all gifted, so that we may make gentle the life of this world and tame the savageness of man.

It is my hope that this collection of wisdom can be given as a gift in the spirit of the Lord. Amen.

ACKNOWLEDGEMENTS

The lecture upon which this book is based came about thanks to many years of study and the wonderful generosity of those who taught me. I first must thank my mentors in matters of religion: Fr. Jeb P. Mayzik, S.J, PhD, Bellarmine University; Rev. Allison F. Gryzlik, St. John's Everett Episcopal Church, the Episcopal Diocese of Tamos; Bishop Sergio J. Shrevtoli, United States Alliance of Catholic Bishops; Rev. Franklin Jung, National Association of Evangelicals; Br. David Sather Mills, C.F.X, Mary Immaculate Center; Bishop Anissa Jackson-Wilkie, Christian Methodist Episcopalian (CME) Church, National Association of Churches; Dan Columbus, President of the Family Faith Council (FFC); Sarah Green, senior pastor of New Hope Christian Center in Alopos, Florida; Spencer Belknap, senior pastor of First Baptist Church in Greenville; Albert Walsh Land, Director of the Southern Evangelical Seminary in Galveston.

I have learned so much from these institutions and I thank you from the well of my soul. I must also thank the business and entrepreneurship professors at Hargrove Business School and who helped set me up for success: Jared Warrow, MBA, Pauline University of Louisiana; Ted Botha, MBA, PhD, Stamford College; Ken Roelof, MBA, MacGill University; Jean-Michel Detourneau, MBA, ME, International Academic Conference on Business (IACB); My additional and exhaustive study in entrepreneurship was thanks to the amazing work done at the Y-Combinator Startup School in Silicon Valley, CA.